101 Strategies for Recruiting Success

101 Strategies for Recruiting Success

Where, When, and How to Find the Right People Every Time

Christopher W. Pritchard, SPHR

American Management Association

New York • Atlanta • Brussels • Chicago • Mexico City • San Francisco
Shanghai • Tokyo • Toronto • Washington, D.C.

Special discounts on bulk quantities of AMACOM books are available to corporations, professional associations, and other organizations. For details, contact Special Sales Department, AMACOM, a division of American Management Association, 1601 Broadway, New York, NY 10019.
Tel.: 212-903-8316. Fax: 212-903-8083.
Website: www.amacombooks.org

This publication is designed to provide accurate and authoritative information in regard to the subject matter covered. It is sold with the understanding that the publisher is not engaged in rendering legal, accounting, or other professional service. If legal advice or other expert assistance is required, the services of a competent professional person should be sought.

Library of Congress Cataloging-in-Publication Data

Pritchard, Christopher W., 1954–
    101 strategies for recruiting success : where, when, and how to find the right people every time / Christopher W. Pritchard.
        p. cm.
    Includes index.
    ISBN-10: 0-8144-7407-1 (pbk.)
    ISBN-13: 978-0-8144-7407-5 (pbk.)
    1. Employees—Recruiting. 2. Employee selection. 3. Employment interviewing.
    I. Title. II. Title: One hundred one strategies for recruiting success. III. Title: One hundred and one strategies for recruiting success.

HF5549.5.R44P75   2007
658.3′11—dc22

                                                                    2006012213

Printing number

10 9 8 7 6 5 4 3 2

Dedicated to Sid Kaufman

Contents

ACKNOWLEDGMENTS   xi

INTRODUCTION   1

CHAPTER 1: FIFTEEN STRATEGIES FOR OPERATIONAL SUCCESS   4

Strategy 1: What Is a Recruiter?   4

Strategy 2: The Operational Audit   7

Strategy 3: The Importance of Planning   10

Strategy 4: Training and Development   12

Strategy 5: Simplify   14

Strategy 6: Make the Most of Metrics   17

Strategy 7: Manage Your Vendor Relationships 22

Strategy 8: Understand the Process   26

Strategy 9: Create Challenging Deliverables   28

Strategy 10: Manage Candidate Flow/Routing   29

Strategy 11: Earn Your Seat at the Table   31

Strategy 12: The Customer Satisfaction Survey 33

Strategy 13: Regular Meetings and Reports   35

Strategy 14: Take Off from the Baseline   37

Strategy 15: Organization Charts   39

CHAPTER 2: SUCCESSFUL SOURCING   41

Strategy 16: Media   41

Strategy 17: Outplacement   43

Strategy 18: Career Fairs   44

Strategy 19: Government Resources   46

Strategy 20: Social Services   47

Strategy 21: Professional Journals and Magazines   48

Strategy 22: Associations   50

Strategy 23: Community Resources   53

Strategy 24: Employee Referrals   55

Strategy 25: Company Alumni   57

Strategy 26: College and University Recruiting   59

Strategy 27: Alumni Associations   62

Strategy 28: Nontraditional Schools and Programs   64

Strategy 29: Military Outplacement   67

Strategy 30: Research Firms   69

Strategy 31: Contingency Recruiters   71

Strategy 32: Retained Search   73

Strategy 33: Open Houses and Other Planned Events   75

Strategy 34: Competitors   78

Strategy 35: Networking   81

Strategy 36: International Recruiting and Sourcing   83

Strategy 37: Internal Postings and Promotions   85

Strategy 38: Candidate Pipeline   87

Strategy 39: Roadkill   89

Strategy 40: Brainstorm   90

CHAPTER 3: DIVERSITY RECRUITMENT   92

Strategy 41: Attracting and Retaining Diverse Talent   92

CHAPTER 4: HIRING SUCCESS

CHAPTER 4: HIRING SUCCESS   **105**

Strategy 42: Partnering   107
Strategy 43: Planning the Process   109
Strategy 44: Recruiting   117
Strategy 45: The Employment Application Form   123
Strategy 46: The Interview   128
Strategy 47: Collateral Material   132
Strategy 48: Background and Reference Checking   133
Strategy 49: The Offer   135
Strategy 50: Paperwork   136
Strategy 51: Evaluation   138

CHAPTER 5: RETENTION SUCCESS   **140**

Strategy 52: Onboarding   142
Strategy 53: Mentoring   144
Strategy 54: Building a Sense of Community   145
Strategy 55: Recognition and Rewards   146
Strategy 56: Involvement   149
Strategy 57: Training and Development   151
Strategy 58: Keep Your Promises   152
Strategy 59: The Report Card   153
Strategy 60: Performance Appraisals   155
Strategy 61: Just Ask!   157
Strategy 62: Exit Interviews (Revisited)   158
Strategy 63: Golden Handcuffs   159
Strategy 64: Anti-Raiding Strategies   160
Strategy 65: Culture   163
Strategy 66: Environment   164

CHAPTER 6: RECRUITING EXCELLENCE WORKBOOK   **166**

Strategy 67: Conduct a Performance *Self*-Appraisal   167
Strategy 68: Read a Good Book   168
Strategy 69: Schedule Your Next Vacation   169

Strategy 70: Interview Employees for Whom You
Paid a Fee   170

Strategy 71: Meet with Legal Counsel   171

Strategy 72: Write a Thank-You Letter   172

Strategy 73: Take a Walk   173

Strategy 74: Seek Advice   174

Strategy 75: Look in the Mirror   175

Strategy 76: Inspirational Sayings and Posters   176

Strategy 77: Visit the Library   177

Strategy 78: Connect with SHRM   178

Strategy 79: Call a Candidate Who Rejected You   179

Strategy 80: Be a Team Player   180

Strategy 81: Read Your Annual Report   181

Strategy 82: Set a New Goal   182

Strategy 83: Attend a Seminar or Take a Class   183

Strategy 84: Brainstorm   184

Strategy 85: Off-Site Meetings   185

Strategy 86: Take a Loved One to Lunch   186

Strategy 87: Count Your Blessings   187

Strategy 88: Interview a Client   188

Strategy 89: Fill Out an Application   189

Strategy 90: Visit Your Company's Website   190

Strategy 91: Visit a Competitor's Website   191

Strategy 92: Visit Internet Job Sites   192

Strategy 93: Interview Other Recruiters   193

Strategy 94: Visit a Career Fair   194

Strategy 95: Critique Your Tools   195

Strategy 96: Study Time Management   196

Strategy 97: Plan Your Day   197

Strategy 98: Seek Out a Mentor   198

Strategy 99: Be a Mentor   199

Strategy 100: Conduct an Operational Audit   200

Strategy 101: Take These Lessons to Heart   201

INDEX   203

Acknowledgments

I wish to thank the following family, friends, and associates for their love, inspiration, and support. Thank you Gayle; you are the love of my life. Your creativity, intelligence, caring, and dedication never cease to amaze me. Thanks to Haley and Brian; I adore you both and am so very proud to be your father. Haley, you are a beautiful woman and always my "magic" baby—a gifted, gentle, and giving soul. Thank you Brian—my best pal. I am humbled by your talent and passion. Thanks Mom and Dad for life, love, and encouragement throughout the years. I am blessed to be your son. I am also grateful to Lou Revnyak, my stepfather, friend, and the best man I have ever known. Thank you Marni, Tim, and Pete for believing in me. Each of you have inspired me by your unwavering commitment to excellence and "making a difference" in all you do and the lives you touch. Thanks to my precious "dancin' guy," Benjamin Louis Pritchard (and your parents Brian and Lindsay) for infusing new life into your ever-loving Grandpa.

My heartfelt appreciation also goes out to: L. Gordon Watson and Rachel Milligan Watson; Olin Rea Pritchard and Margaret Banning Pritchard; Joan, Kathy, Amy, and Adam Pritchard; Ray C. Sharp III; Specialist William Carroll; Bob Amos; Kurt and Barb Musser; James and Melinda Cumpton; Jim Weldon; FIPC and Life Group; the BVU; Jack Wessel; Hank Linderman; Barb Beath; Tony Sharp; Ed Lessin; Ted Kempel; Mark Wyar; BackBay, a.k.a. "The Lads"; Frank and Cynthia Longstreth; Ruth Rousch; Ruth Eggleton; Arthur and Louis Stern; Steve Magyar; Mike Molloy; Larry Chung; Gint Baukus; my associates at Sales Consultants, LDI, National City Corporation, and Schumacher Homes; and the many others who have so generously blessed and enriched my life.

Last but not least, I wish to express my sincere appreciation to my editor Adrienne Hickey, associate editor Erika Spelman, copyeditor Mary Miller, proofreader Tina Orem, and the rest of the AMACOM team who applied their talent and experience toward making this book the best it could be.

101 Strategies for Recruiting Success

Introduction

I have written this book to support the HR professional who is in dedicated pursuit of recruitment excellence. By definition, mediocrity is the norm. The word *mediocre* is derived from the Latin word *mediocris* meaning "middle." Those who pursue excellence are not satisfied with the middle. They are dedicated to rising above the commonplace to soar with eagles.

Over the course of the past twenty-three years, I have experienced the recruiting profession from a variety of perspectives. In 1983, I went through my baptism of fire as a rookie recruiter at Sid Kaufman's Management Recruiters' (MRI) office in Akron, Ohio. MRI's recruiter-training program taught me how to be an organized, creative, and street-smart professional. It taught me how to make a living in the competitive world of contingency recruiting. Sid Kaufman and his wife, Helene, have my heartfelt gratitude.

In the mid 1980s, I moved to Philadelphia and worked as a part-time research assistant within a respected retained search firm while establishing my own recruiting firm. The retained recruiters I encountered considered themselves a cut above their peers on the contingency side of the business. After spending time on both sides of the retained versus contingency divide, I concluded that any attitude of superiority was unjustified. I proceeded to build my own firm with a blended service model—that is, offering retained and contingency services specific to my clients' needs.

Over the next five years, I enjoyed a great deal of success as a trainer and manager of recruiters. Throughout this time, I personally worked on a wide variety of recruiting assignments to keep my own recruitment skills sharp. Despite many accomplishments, I did not have the general business expertise needed to grow my company. In late 1989, I decided to shut down my entrepreneurial venture to accept an offer of full-time employment with a client company, LDI Corporation, and its young, dynamic, and exceptionally capable president, Michael Joseph. I owe much of my general business education and success to Michael. I will always be grateful for the personal and professional investment he has made in me.

I have spent the better part of the past seventeen years managing recruiting programs inside corporate America. During times of career transition, I have relied on my recruiting street smarts to earn a living as a consultant to companies such as General Electric, Coopers & Lybrand, Ernst and Young, Lotus Development Corporation, Dell Corporation, Boeing Corporation, and The May Company, among others.

I have endeavored to weave personal and professional lessons learned into the fabric of this book. I've divided 101 strategies for recruitment success among a half-dozen topics of discussion. Chapter 1 offers insight into general recruiting operations through fifteen specific strategies. Chapter 2 is a goldmine of hard-hitting techniques regarding when, where, and how to find the right candidate. I trust you will find these twenty-five strategies an eye-opening and challenging introduction to outside-the-box recruitment sourcing. Chapter 3 advocates less talk and more action in this common sense–based approach to diversity-minded recruitment and retention. Chapter 4 features ten strategies for successful hiring. We'll take a constructively critical look at hiring processes and procedures within the typical U.S. corporation. Chapter 5 explores fifteen strategies to encourage retention within our organizations. We are often guilty of focusing all our recruitment-related energies on welcoming new employees in the front door while disregarding the hemorrhaging of experienced employees out the back door. Optimal recruitment success is undermined anytime we fail to retain the employees we already have. Finally, Chapter 6 encourages practical application of lessons learned in the first five chapters via thirty-five strategic exercises.

I'm looking forward to sharing the journey with you. Roll up your sleeves and let's get started!

CHAPTER 1

Fifteen Strategies for Operational Success

▲ Strategy 1: What Is a Recruiter?

Answering this question is a critical first step on the road to recruiting success. As the newly hired vice president of recruiting for a $100 billion-plus public company, I initiated a series of one-on-one meetings with the members of my recruiting team. I wanted to get to know each one of my recruiters and assess his or her individual strengths and weaknesses. I found each individual to be personable, intelligent, and dedicated. I was nonetheless concerned when I learned that the majority of the team had been placed into human resources and recruiting roles by way of administrative positions that had been eliminated. In other words, when management couldn't find anything else for these people to do, they concluded, "Let's put them in recruiting."

Corporate America often thinks of recruiting as an administrative process that has the following duties:

- Filling out a requisition form and entering it into the Human Resource Information System (HRIS)
- Running advertisements in the newspaper or on the Internet
- Waiting for the résumés to start rolling in
- Screening résumés for key words found in the requisition
- Conducting initial phone screens
- Scheduling interviews with the hiring manager
- Sending out offer and rejection letters

Were this scenario to accurately reflect the world of recruiting, former administrators should make ideal recruiters.

In reality, former administrators may or may not make excellent recruiters. The key to answering the question "What is a recruiter?" begs the larger question: "What should our recruiting processes look like?" Once we have defined the term *optimal recruiting,* we can define the optimal recruiter. Rather than answering these questions at this time, I will let the answers emerge from our examination of all 101 strategies for recruiting success. As we progress through this book, it will become apparent that my personal view of recruiting does not follow the aforementioned administrative model. My model brings the following characteristics to mind:

- Creative
- Sales aptitude and interest
- Personable
- Assertive

- Excellent communication skills

- Excellent listening skills

- Attention to detail/organized

- Dedicated/passionate/driven

- Intelligent

Recruiters are the organization's gatekeepers. A candidate's first impression of an organization and its specific employment opportunities are greatly influenced by the recruiter. Recruiter creativity, dedication, and expertise make all the difference between finding the best available talent and finding simply readily available talent. Think about it. Who is managing the gate at your organization? The gatekeeper's competence will affect the number and quality of candidates sourced. This, in turn, will affect the number and quality of hires made, and, ultimately, the quality of the company itself. Has your company entrusted this role to recruiters or administrative order-takers?

Food for Thought: I once encountered a company that entrusted its recruitment practice to low-level (and low-paid) administrative order-takers. This same company paid millions of dollars to third-party recruiting firms each year. The average fee was $25,000 per placement! A multibillion-dollar third-party recruiting industry has evolved as outside recruiters (well trained and well paid) get the job done for poorly trained and poorly paid internal recruiting personnel. What is wrong with this picture?

▲ **Strategy 2:** The Operational Audit

Before meaningful change can be planned and implemented, we must understand the existing state of affairs. A comprehensive audit of recruiting policies, procedures, tools, and personnel should be undertaken to determine departmental strengths and weaknesses. I recommend a thorough investigation into every aspect of current recruiting operations, such as:

Workflow

- How is a new requisition opened?
- What documentation is required?
- What authorization is needed?
- How are requisitions assigned to specific recruiters?
- How are open requisitions and recruiting activities prioritized?
- What administrative procedures are involved, such as employment, applications, HRIS entry, offer/rejection letters, and so forth?
- How are candidates sourced?
- How are candidates screened to verify level of qualification?
- How are candidates introduced to the hiring manager?
- How or when do hiring managers provide feedback to recruiters?
- How are hiring decisions made?
- Who is authorized to make a hiring decision?
- Who handles reference and background checks?

- How is an offer or rejection letter communicated to candidates?

Competency

- What metrics exist regarding current levels of performance?
- How much does the company rely on outside recruiters? Why?
- What would a customer satisfaction survey reveal?
- Are some recruiters more successful than others? Why?

Support

- What is the recruiting department's budget? If one exists, is it sufficient?
- Are budgeted monies being spent wisely? How is cost-effectiveness measured?
- What administrative support is available for recruiters?
- What systems and tools are available?
- Do recruiters have a "seat at the table" at client departmental/staff meetings?
- Examine overall communication patterns between recruiters and clients. How do these communication patterns facilitate or hamper success?
- How are recruiters compensated, recognized, and rewarded?
- How are recruiters challenged?

- Do recruiters receive adequate training and development?

- Are recruiters given specific goals and objectives?

- How are recruiter performance appraisals handled? When and how?

These are some of the questions that should be answered. I encourage you to add to this list. Dig, and then dig some more. Organizations often fail to excel because they fail to take a constructively critical look at the way they do things. Work toward achieving both big picture and detailed perspective. Be constructively critical. I promise you, the operational audit will be an eye-opening experience. Open and honest self-examination is a well-established best practice of champions.

▲ **Strategy 3:** The Importance of Planning

It is a clichéd but true saying that "when you fail to plan, you plan to fail." Recruiting is too often a reactive rather than a pro-active process. In many organizations, recruiters do not have a seat at the planning table. Whenever this is the case, a recruiter's ability to proactively anticipate client needs is unnecessarily and unwisely compromised. Clients deliver requisitions out of the blue with an "I needed this person yesterday" attitude. Recruiters scramble to deliver a warm body to yet another requisition of unanticipated urgency. It is a setup for failure. Recruitment planning should include the following:

- Regular discussions with clients to anticipate future hiring needs

- Development of proactive candidate pipelines for critical skill sets

- Maintenance of a network of contacts (candidates, employees, competitors, and so forth)

- Development and maintenance of a strong employee referral program

- Cooperation with management to ensure adequate budget

- Strategic and tactical flexibility and creativity

- Investment in recruiter training and development

When you break the pattern of reactive recruiting, your life will be easier. You will be under less pressure. You will be more deliberate and efficient. As a result, you will tend to be more time- and cost-effective than you ever could be while engaged in a "ready, shoot, aim" approach to recruitment. You will dramatically increase the likelihood of finding and attracting the best available candidates.

Recruiting managers should use weekly staff meetings to ask recruiters the following questions:

- What new requisitions are on the horizon?
- What steps have you taken to build your candidate pipeline?
- What assistance do you need?
- What obstacles are you facing?

Recruiters need encouragement, guidance, and partnering from management. They need to know that management is committed to facilitating proactive (rather than reactive) recruiting. They need to know that management is committed to supporting them in any and every way necessary to ensure success.

▲ **Strategy 4:** Training and Development

Prior to picking up this book, when was the last time you read a book about recruiting? Do you know the names Tony Byrne, Michael Bloch, or Bill Radin (among others in the recruiter training profession)? Have you heard of the *Fordyce Letter*? Do you belong to the Society for Human Resource Management (SHRM)? Have you participated in SHRM's Employment Management Association (EMA) over the years? Do you attend association meetings and workshops? If not, why not?

I'm hard pressed to think of a single professional athlete who does not maintain a strict training and development regimen. We trust that our doctors, our lawyers, our tax accountants, and our commercial airline pilots invest appropriate time and effort to ensure that their professional skills remain sharp and up-to-date. We expect this of virtually every professional we encounter. Indeed, an ongoing commitment to training and development is an essential characteristic of anyone appropriately called a *professional*. Oddly, we are often remiss in our commitment to training and development within our recruitment departments. Why is this?

PROBLEM: budgetary constraints. Most organizations view recruitment as a cost center (that is, overhead). During tough economic times, we are asked to tighten our belts and trim expenses.

SOLUTION: Remember the story of the company that paid millions of dollars in recruiting fees each year? I discovered that many of the employees who had been found via outside recruiting firms had previously applied to the company directly. Overworked, undertrained recruiters often make costly errors and inefficiencies. What is the lesson to be learned here?

Failure to train and develop recruiters and recruiting systems will often prove much more costly than training itself. The right answer is to invest in training. Be creative. Find ways to make things happen. When money is tight, there is always the public library. You may also want to establish a departmental library where books and other resource material may be shared.

Too often the real problem is lack of motivation. Where there is a will, there is always a way.

▲ **Strategy 5:** Simplify

I believe in following the KISS rule: Keep It Simple, Stupid! It is foolish indeed to make things unnecessarily complicated. The recruiting professional's world has its fair share of complexity. We do not have the luxury of simply finding and hiring the best available candidate. We must also be sensitive to the demands of legal compliance and litigation-avoidance concerns. Fortunately, amid an ocean of operational and administrative minutiae, there are islands of opportunity for us to simplify our efforts.

Every recruiting project should begin with an examination of what I like to refer to as the "low-hanging fruit." Before time, effort, and expense are invested in extensive search activities, re-cruiters should ask themselves the following questions:

- Are there any viable internal candidates?
- Are there any viable external candidates already in our files?
- Might my network of personal contacts help me identity the right candidate?
- Is there a simple and direct source that I am overlooking?

A nationally respected Fortune 500 company recently paid more than $75,000 in fees to third-party recruiters for the place-ment of four candidates who were available to its internal recruiters on a direct (no-fee) basis. Specifically, two of the can-didates had previously applied to the company. Their résumés were readily available via in-house files had anyone bothered to look. The other two candidates had posted their résumés to an Internet résumé bank. The company had paid a hefty annual fee for direct-access rights to this same résumé bank. Again, no one had bothered to look.

Do you have an effective/efficient information storage and retrieval system? You should be able to access any given résumé in your files by using a simple keyword database inquiry. There are plenty of fancy and expensive ways to accomplish this task. When budget dollars are tight, I suggest you look into linking an inexpensive scanner to an inexpensive relational database with optical character recognition (OCR) functionality. Expert members of relational-database user groups are readily available to help you create an effective and inexpensive solution. Contact your local MS Access, FoxPro, Oracle or other relational database software user group in your area for assistance. Adequate data storage and retrieval solutions are often available for less money than you would spend on a single third-party recruiter placement fee because you couldn't find information within your own records.

Is your HRIS applicant-tracking system recruiter friendly? Recruiters can become bogged down with administrative tasks such as HRIS data entry. Although it is important to track data, I strongly advise that you analyze the amount of time your recruiters spend keypunching. Look for ways to work with your information technology (IT) department to simplify data-capture processes. You should also make every effort to simplify the type and amount of data that you enter. For example, a yes/no box would suffice for educational data. You might even assume "no" whenever "yes" has not been checked, as on the sample candidate list in Figure 1-1.

In this example, keypunching the X key three times is easier and less time-consuming than typing the name and address of each school attended, subject matter studied, grade point aver-

FIGURE 1-1. SIMPLIFICATION OF DATA ENTRY.

Have you earned any of the following degrees? (Check all that apply)

High School Diploma or GED: X

Bachelor of Arts or Science: X

Master of Business Administration: X

Masters (other than MBA): _____

Ph.D.: _____

Note: Harvard MBA 1987

ages earned, and the month and year of each graduation. If or when there is something especially noteworthy; it may be placed in a "notes" section. Take a hard look at your systems and procedures. Ask yourself the following questions:

- Is this task necessary?

- Do we really need to track this particular type of data?

- Does each task and system function do what we want it to do?

- Is there a simpler or more efficient way of accomplishing this task?

Keep things simple. Remember, more keypunching equals less recruiting.

▲ **Strategy 6:** Make the Most of Metrics

Cost-per-hire refers to total costs associated with all hiring activities divided by the total number of hires. In other words, add up the cost of recruiters' compensation (pay and benefits) plus all advertising costs, agency fees, employee-referral fees, candidate travel, lodging, entertainment, relocation costs, and any/all additional costs associated with your hiring process. Then, divide the sum of these dollars by the total number of hires you have made. For example:

Total cost: $1,237,450
Total hires: 220
Cost-per-hire: $5,624.77

This may then be used as a benchmark against which to reduce cost-per-hire overtime. Cost-reduction begins by answering questions such as the following:

- Where is the money being spent?

- Are there any obvious areas where we can reduce or eliminate costs?

- Can we negotiate a better deal with our recruiting vendors (20 percent rather than 25 percent fees)?

- Can we trim airfare expenses by planning ahead (for example, fourteen-day advance ticketing)?

- Can we cut a better deal with regard to lodging?

- Will our preferred vendors give us a deeper discount if we use them exclusively?

- Are there other vendors we should approach for competitive bids?
- Can we run fewer or smaller ads without compromising results?
- Did we get any viable candidates from our participation in the three local career fairs that we participated in so far this year?
- Does one Internet job board tend to yield more or better candidates than another?

Were we to trim $250,000 off of the previous sample costs, while making the same number of hires, our cost-per-hire would look like this:

Total cost: $987,450
Total hires: 220
Cost-per-hire: $4,488.41

Moving our cost-per-hire from $5,624.77 to $4,488.41 is a 20 percent savings. Needless to say, senior management would love this savings.

Days-to-fill refers to the total number of days that requisitions were open *divided* by the total number of requisitions filled. For example: Chart each requisition with its respective days-to-fill data (see Figure 1-2).

Here is where things get a bit tricky. If we take the arithmetic mean of the numbers in our days-to-fill column (20 + 38 + 98 + 20 + 42), we arrive at an average of 44 days-to-fill—that is, 218 divided by 5 = 43.6.

A fundamental class in statistics would teach us that *average* is a relative term:

FIGURE 1-2. SAMPLE "DAYS-TO-FILL"
DATASHEET.

Requisition #	Date Opened	Date Closed	Days-to-Fill
12345	1/2/07	1/23/07	20
12346	1/6/07	2/12/07	38
12347	1/7/07	4/14/07	98
12349	1/15/07	2/3/07	20
12350	1/27/07	3/9/07	42

- The *mean* days-to-fill is 44.
- The *median* days-to-fill is 38.
- The *mode* days-to-fill is 20.

Any of these may legitimately be called the average.

Note what happens to our chart in Figure 1-3 when we subtract weekends and holidays from the days-to-fill column.

FIGURE 1-3. ALTERNATIVE "DAYS-TO-FILL"
DATASHEET.

Requisition #	Date Opened	Date Closed	Days-to-Fill minus weekends and holidays
12345	1/2/07	1/23/07	13
12346	1/6/07	2/12/07	26
12347	1/7/07	4/14/07	78
12349	1/15/07	2/3/07	13
12350	1/27/07	3/9/07	31

The date-opened and the date-filled columns remain exactly the same. However, once we subtract nonworking days from our days-to-fill column, our average time drops to a more realistic look at the actual workdays it took to fill each opening:

- The *mean* days-to-fill drops from 44 to 32 days.

- The *median* days-to-fill drops from 38 to 26 days.

- The *mode* days-to-fill drops from 20 to 13 days.

Which numbers are the most accurate indicator of days-to-fill? Which numbers would you rather present to your boss?

We can look at the exact same data through a variety of lenses. Variance between the three types of averaging (mean, median, and mode) can be dramatic when dealing with a small statistical population. For example, if a recruiter takes 20 days to fill 10 positions and 180 days to fill 1 particularly difficult position, the mean would be 34.5 days. In this instance, the small population (11) allows the highest individual day-to-fill number (180) to significantly influence the arithmetic mean.

Let's assume the position that stayed open for 180 days was one where the hiring manager kept changing her mind regarding exactly what she was looking for (ever happened to you?). Under these circumstances, the mode (20 days) most accurately reflects average performance. With this in mind, we need to exercise care in selecting the averaging formula that most accurately reflects performance. We may wish to subtract the day that the requisition was opened and/or the day it was filled from the total number of days open. We may consider freezing the days-to-fill clock when a recruiter is stuck waiting for feedback from the hiring manager. For example, a recruiter may have located and introduced the candidate that is ultimately hired within a few days or weeks. That recruiter should not have his days-to-fill record adversely affected by hiring-decision delays that are beyond his control.

Additional metrics such as *submissions-to-candidates, candi-*

dates-to-hires, and others (be creative) may be used to monitor specific aspects of performance. For example, suppose that only one in every ten candidates submitted by a particular recruiter to a specific hiring manager is accepted as a viable candidate. This metric suggests that recruiter and hiring manager are not on the same page of the playbook regarding their understanding of what constitutes a "qualified" candidate. In such a case, a submission-to-candidate ratio may bring difficulties to light and encourage corrective action. Let metrics work for you.

▲ **Strategy 7:** Manage Your Vendor Relationships

In-house recruiters typically have little or no familiarity with the world of their counterparts in outside (third-party) recruiting organizations. This being the case, they may be vulnerable to establishing and/or maintaining agreements that are not in their own (or their company's) best interest. In this tail-wagging-the-dog scenario, vendors dictate the terms and conditions to the customer.

I'd like to make the following recommendations for your consideration:

1. Have a *Very* Compelling Reason Before Using a Retained Search Firm

Retained firms are typically your most expensive recruiting option (often 35 percent of total compensation plus search-related expenses). As you know, retained search firms are paid regardless of the results generated. This may be the way to go when you have an especially high-level search and/or a need to ensure utmost confidentiality. You may also want to ensure the door-opening power of an internationally recognized name because access to the world's most powerful executives is highly restricted.

Having personally worked within retained and contingency search firms, I honestly believe that any contingency-based recruiter worth his or her salt will be able to deliver equal quality of candidates and turnaround time. The contingency recruiter's services will yield significant cost savings 99 percent of the time.

2. Don't Pay More Than Necessary

I know that 30 percent contingency fees (and higher) are not unusual. As a general rule, you need not pay them. I spent approximately ten years of my career as a third-party recruiter. As a general rule, 25 percent is the most you should pay. When you have multiple searches (even if they are spread out over time), you should receive volume-discount consideration. I have negotiated dozens of third-party recruiting agreements at 15 percent fee levels without compromising the number or quality of candidate submissions. I've negotiated higher and lower fees over the years as warranted by the unique aspects of the searches assigned to me. In most instances, I believe 20 percent is the right number. Believe it or not, most agencies will stand in line for a shot at your business on a 20 percent contingency fee basis. Any agency that tells you otherwise is playing a hardball sales game that you need not buy into. If you respond, as I have, they'll generally come around: "I'm not trying to sell you or twist your arm here. I realize that a 20 percent fee may not be consistent with your company's business model. That being the case, I'll respect your decision not to work with me at this time. I'm simply saying that *my* business model dictates that I restrict my approved third-party vendor list to recruiting firms that charge no higher than a 20 percent fee." **Note:** Watch out for additional costs or fees based on total realistic first-year earnings. There are plenty of recruiters that will restrict their fees to a percentage of base-salary only.

You will often receive a longwinded rebuttal regarding why and how your 20 percent position hurts *you*. You will we warned about reduced quality of candidates, reduced vendor commitment, and "blah . . . blah . . . blah." Don't believe it! Hold firm.

When the whining and posturing are over, most recruiters interested in a long-term relationship with you will accommodate a 20 percent model. If you allow yourself the flexibility of paying "as much as 20 percent," you will have plenty of vendors to choose from. You can also take advantage of better deals when available. Many companies offer 17.5 percent fees (and lower). Should a specific search warrant a higher fee on your part—treat it as the exception rather than the rule.

3. Set Your Own Contractual Terms

Finally, make sure that the contracts governing your agreements with any or all recruiting vendors are *your* contracts. Be sure to work with a qualified attorney when developing any contract. You will need to clarify fees, guarantee period, confidentiality, and indemnification clauses governing law, term, and severability clauses and a variety of additional terms and conditions. Among other specifications, you should state:

- You will not accept unsolicited résumés from the outside recruiting vendor.
- Vendor's personnel will not contact or communicate directly with anyone within your company other than designated human resources personnel unless expressly authorized by you to do so.
- Vendor will not recruit, solicit for employment, or initiate recruitment of any of your employees for positions outside of your company during the term of your agreement and thereafter for a period of twelve (or more) months.
- If the vendor should present a candidate for a specific position and you are already aware of that same candidate's

availability (via a prior source), then the vendor's claim to representation of such candidate will not be accepted.

- For each valid candidate presented by the vendor, you will be required to pay the placement fee only in the event that your company hires the candidate within one year immediately following vendor's presentation.

- If the same candidate is presented to your organization by more than one recruitment agency, each vendor agrees that you will honor the *first* presentation of the candidate as verified by your HR/recruiter's time-stamped receipt. This will be the only valid claim to candidate representation for purposes of placement fee payment.

Use appropriate legal counsel and craft an agreement that protects your company via clarification of all terms and conditions.

▲ Strategy 8: Understand the Process

It is helpful to map your recruiting processes as a formal flow chart. The previously mentioned operational audit will help you secure most of the information needed to build such a map:

Opening the Requisition

- How is a requisition opened?
- What documentation is required?
- What authorization is needed?
- Where and to whom is each newly approved requisition routed?
- How are requisitions assigned to particular recruiters?
- How is requisition workload prioritized?
- What administrative procedures are involved?

Sourcing Processes

- How are candidates sourced?
- Are jobs posted internally (when and by whom)?
- How does the Employee Referral Program receive notification?
- Who decides if/when to run an advertisement?
- What are the authorized spending limits?
- Who decides if/when to engage outside recruiters?

Candidate Screening and Introduction

- How are candidates screened?
- Who is responsible for initial screening?
- How are viable candidates introduced to the hiring manager?

- When candidates fail initial screening, who is responsible for rejection letters?

Interview and Hire Protocols

- Who is responsible for interview scheduling and travel arrangements?
- How are hiring or rejection decisions made?
- How/When do hiring managers provide feedback to recruiters?
- Who is authorized to make a hiring decision?
- Who handles reference and background checks?
- How is an offer or rejection communicated to a candidate?
- Who is responsible for making sure that formal application has been made?

Closing the Requisition

- Who ensures I-9, W-2, payroll/benefit, and other documentation has been completed and appropriately routed or filed?
- Who is responsible for new-hire onboarding processes?
- Who is responsible for closing out the requisition?

Take time to create a formal work-flow chart or manual. With this visual map of how things are *supposed* to work, you can increase the likelihood that things will actually run according to plan. A process map facilitates identification of glitches and/or the need for improvement.

▲ **Strategy 9:** Create Challenging Deliverables

Too often recruiting departments operate without clearly stated objectives. We make ambiguous statements such as the following:

- "This requisition may take weeks to fill, maybe even months. It's hard to tell."
- "We make no promises."
- "We'll give it our best shot."
- "We'll try to contain costs but they will be what they will be."

Without clear performance targets, outcomes are determined strictly by chance. For those recruiters who truly wish to excel, I strongly recommend specific and "shared" (that is, "communicated") objectives. Let your clients know what you are going to do for them, then work to make it happen. For example, you might say:

- "We will submit no less than three viable candidates within ten working days."
- "We will reduce cost-per-hire by 30 percent over last year's numbers."
- "We will reduce reliance on outside recruiting vendors by 50 percent over last year's numbers."

Choose your deliverables wisely. Don't overcommit, but don't *under*commit either. Stretch your recruiters to their highest level of performance. Create a fun and challenging team environment so that you can "wow" your customers.

▲ **Strategy 10:** Manage Candidate Flow/Routing

A recruiter recently told me that he had received more than one thousand résumés in response to an advertisement he had placed on the Internet. Tough economic times create a supply/demand imbalance with more candidates than jobs available. In good times and bad, recruiters must address candidate flow and routing concerns. When hundreds or thousands of résumés arrive at once, e-mail accounts may fill to capacity and begin to reject additional e-mail; physical management of snail-mail résumés may strain administrative resources. In such cases, identification of qualified candidates may be delayed or missed all together. Needless to say, it can be very disruptive to a recruiter's day when her personal inbox has reached the limit of its capacity. Reading, sorting, and responding to candidate inquiries can become a full-time job. I recommend the following:

• Ask your IT team or ISP-provider to set up special e-mail accounts so that resumes arrive in prerouted mailboxes. For example, résumés submitted in response to an advertisement for a credit manager could be routed to an e-mail account such as CreditManager@yourcompany.com. Access to this account would be restricted to designated recruiters and administrative personnel. Résumé flow/routing could then be managed at a pace set by those with access. Should overwhelming numbers of résumés arrive at any given time, a temporary worker can be assigned to assist with screening and routing duties. Only résumés meeting specific criteria would be forwarded to designated recruiters for further screening. Those not meeting specific criteria could be e-mailed preapproved response letters and their résumés filed.

- When an overwhelming response is anticipated, it is wise to consider outsourcing. In other words, utilize a research firm or temporary agency to provide low-cost services related to initial screening activities (ad placement, gathering résumés, and screening for specific keywords and qualifications). A so-called blind advertisement may be placed on your behalf. A blind advertisement does not reveal your company name: "*Our Client* is seeking a vice president of human resources with the following credentials and experience . . . Please send résumés to Outsourcing Vendor at P.O. Box 123." This way you would not have to worry about responding to (or storing) a thousand résumés.

I am all for the elimination of busywork and inefficiency whenever and wherever possible. An attitude of "this is the way we've always done things" is a one-way ticket to mediocrity. Creative and intelligent minds look at each situation and ask, "Is there a better way to handle this?" Don't let another day go by on autopilot.

▲ Strategy 11: Earn Your Seat at the Table

Among the many HR buzz terms du jour is the ever-elusive *seat at the table.* This is a clever term for building and maintaining optimal working relationships. Optimal relationships are built on open and honest communication and on mutual trust and respect. They are partnerships in which each partner is committed to keeping the other in the loop regarding problems as well as progress toward shared goals.

The typical recruiting department does not have a seat at the table. It is uninvolved in the day-to-day world of its clients. Likewise, its clients have little awareness or appreciation for the world of recruiting. I believe the best way to overcome such isolation is to take an active and genuine interest in learning more about the clients' worlds.

Crawl into each client's world by doing the following:

- Ask if you may attend an occasional staff meeting to develop a deeper appreciation of the day-to-day issues and future directions your client faces. A "fly on the wall" presence can be very educational.

- Ask if you can be added to the distribution list of staff meeting minutes from each of your key client groups.

- Ask key clients to provide you with the names of the associations they belong to, and the professional journals, magazines, and Internet sources that help them stay on top of developments within their respective professions. Take time to familiarize yourself with these same resources to become more knowledgeable and conversant in your clients' worlds.

- Invest personal one-on-one time with your clients. Invite clients out for an occasional cup of coffee or lunch just to catch up on what is new in their worlds. Express an interest in your clients' personal lives as well as their professional lives.

If you take time to understand more about your clients' worlds you will be better prepared to search for appropriate candidates and recognize them when you find them. If you understand the responsibilities and challenges that your clients face, you will enhance your ability to anticipate hiring needs and to establish proactive candidate pipelines. You will find that your clients really appreciate your efforts. Their respect for your opinion will be enhanced. You will be perceived as a knowledgeable and valued member of the team.

You will have earned your seat at the table.

▲ Strategy 12: The Customer Satisfaction Survey

Regular feedback from clients is essential to recruiting success. Feedback can be gathered from informal one-on-one contacts such as a meeting, an e-mail, or on the telephone. It can be as simple as asking a client a few straightforward questions, such as the following:

- "Are we getting the job done that you expect/hope from us?"
- "How well are our efforts meeting your needs?"
- "How might we improve?"

Many recruiting departments tend to unnecessarily formalize this procedure. Questionnaires are sent out with the typical language: "Please rate the recruiting department on each of the following performance variables using a scale of 1 to 10 (1 = very poor and 10 = superior performance)."

We need to appreciate that our clients do not generally welcome yet another piece of paperwork on their desks. In my experience, only the rare client invests the time and effort to thoughtfully answer our questionnaires. Many will zip through a survey as quickly and perfunctorily as possible just to get it off their "to do" lists.

Don't get me wrong. I recognize the value of formal surveys. When making a state-of-recruiting-department address to senior management, I'd rather have empirical data at my fingertips than fuzzy statements such as "I've talked to a few of my clients and they seem to be very satisfied." Still, I believe we will secure our most meaningful feedback by way of informal, ongoing, and relationship-driven communication with our clients.

We need not (and should not) wait for the yearly *formal* survey to tell us how we are doing. Every now and then, test the waters. Let your clients know that you are genuinely concerned about their satisfaction at all times (not only when the annual customer satisfaction survey goes out).

Finally, give your clients a break from lengthy and complex surveys. When you informally track customer satisfaction throughout the year, you will already have an ongoing source of feedback to guide you toward success. I believe the formal customer satisfaction survey should include only two questions:

Question #1: Are you *Very Satisfied* _____, *Somewhat Satisfied* _____, or *Dissatisfied* _____ with the recruiting department's efforts on your behalf? (Check one.)

Question #2: How might we improve?

Strategy 13: Regular Meetings and Reports

I am a rather zealous proponent of an open-door policy and frequent (albeit brief) meetings to maintain strong lines of communication. I believe in closely monitoring the progress (or lack thereof) being made on every open requisition by asking the following questions:

- How many new candidates have been introduced this week?

- Where have we found these candidates?

- Where will we look for additional candidates if needed?

- How many have been screened and are ready for their interviews?

- What feedback have we received to date from the hiring manager?

- How close are we to a hiring decision?

- What anticipated and unanticipated obstacles can we think of that may get in the way of successfully filling this requisition?

- What can we do to avoid or overcome these obstacles?

Note: Having personally directed national recruiting teams with hundreds of open requisitions, I appreciate that it is not always possible for any one person to monitor this level of detail. In such instances, I hold recruitment managers accountable for the status of requisitions assigned to their particular team of recruiters. This field data may be readily summarized and rolled up to senior management. I secure the specific data that I choose to monitor (such as numbers, sources, or who/what/when/where) via daily open-door communication, coupled with weekly staff meetings and regular reports. I use regular meetings and reports to encourage creative thinking and problem solving. I want to create a sense teamwork and urgency by stressing the following:

- Let's think!
- Let's move!
- Let's work together to make things happen!
- Let's get these requisitions across the finish line!

▲ **Strategy 14:** Take Off from the Baseline

As mentioned earlier, I believe in the importance of having specific objectives toward reaching your goal of recruiting excellence. I refer to these objectives as *target deliverables*—an unambiguous declaration of exactly what we're going to do for our clients. I believe in setting high, yet realistic, expectations so as to challenge recruiters without inviting failure and disappointment. This balancing act rests on a fulcrum of baseline performance, as shown in Figure 1-4.

Use baseline measurements as your springboard to improved performance. For example, calculate quarterly days-to-fill and then challenge the team to improve on that baseline number in the coming quarter. Utilize team recognition ceremonies, plaques, and fun gifts or prizes to help motivate your team. Do the same with any or all performance variables that you wish to improve upon, including the following:

• *Cost-per-Hire.* Challenge your team members to reduce reliance on outside recruiting vendors. Challenge them to conduct a thorough search of existing résumés and employee referrals before running expensive ads. Challenge them to concentrate on

FIGURE 1-4. PERFORMANCE IS MEASURED FROM THE BASELINE.

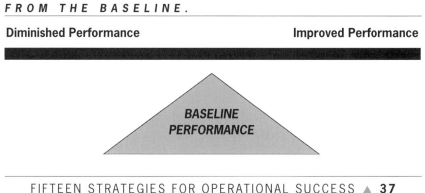

Diminished Performance   Improved Performance

BASELINE
PERFORMANCE

local market candidates to avoid expensive travel and relocation expenses.

• *Submission-to-Hire Ratio.* If your team submits ten candidates on average before one hire is made, challenge your team to work closely with hiring managers to improve performance from 10:1 to 5:1, or better.

• *Offer-to-Acceptance Ratio.* Challenge your team to become more fully engaged in the offer process. When recruiters pay close attention to a candidate's buying signals, they may anticipate problems and address them before they arise. If eight out of ten offers are accepted, shoot for nine out of ten or ten out of ten. Have fun and challenge your team with incremental improvement targets.

▲ **Strategy 15:** Organization Charts

Knowing "who does what" and "who reports to whom" within our own organizations is an important aspect of recruiting success. Complex organizational structures demand road maps to help us achieve an adequate understanding of the lay of the land.

Organization charts (org-charts) are common but often underutilized tools. I believe it wise to attach a client's org-chart to each open requisition. This will help you place open positions in their organizational context. It will help you screen out under-qualified or overqualified applicants, and it will help you sell the opportunity to qualified candidates. Regular exposure to org-charts also furthers your efforts to understand your client's world and earn a seat at the table.

Org-charts are also useful when you need additional insight into specific position orders. Familiarity with departmental structure may prove invaluable when you want to identify an existing employee in a similar position who may provide you with additional insight into the open requisition. *Note:* Be sure to coordinate such employee contact with the hiring manager so as not to step on his or her toes in the process.

I like to ask managers, "If you could clone one or more employees who excel at the type of work your new employee will be doing, who would you choose to clone?" I then suggest that it would be helpful for me to spend fifteen to twenty minutes with those individuals to seek their input. Again, I recommend asking these individuals about the associations they belong to and the professional journals, magazines, and Internet sources that help them stay on top of developments in their profession.

Ask the hiring manager and others within his or her org-chart the following questions:

- Where would you look for this individual if you were in my shoes?

- What does a typical day consist of for someone in this position?

- If you found the perfect candidate, how would you sell this opportunity? In other words, why would someone want to work with you? What about this opportunity makes it exceptional?

Organization charts can spark ideas. They can direct you to the appropriate parties for additional input and advice. Org-charts can help you make each search come alive.

CHAPTER 2

Successful Sourcing

▲ Strategy 16: Media

Recruiters have long relied on the classified section of their local newspapers to advertise open requisitions. Newspaper advertisements fall into the "It's the way we've always done things" category. I'm not knocking newspaper ads. I would like to suggest, however, that newspaper advertising (along with other sourcing techniques) be evaluated for cost-effectiveness:

- If you run a $5,000 advertisement, are the results better than a $500 advertisement—that is, did you get more and/ or better quality candidates?

- How many hires may be directly attributed to the specific advertisement?

- Does one newspaper tend to yield better results than another?

- Have you looked into negotiating better rates (such as volume discounts or special offers)?

- Have you compared newspaper results to other media? Use of radio or television is generally kept to a minimum because of cost constraints.

- Have you compared the cost, readership demographics, and distribution specifications of one newspaper against those of another?

Let's say you ran a $500 advertisement and it generated one hundred responses from which you ultimately hired four new employees. This is a 25:1 applicant to hire ratio. It also translates into $125 of advertising cost per candidate hired.

When you spend under $1,000 for an advertisement, even a single hire generally justifies the cost. When you have spent significant dollars for a display ad, make sure that you take time to analyze your bang for the buck. Newspaper and advertising agencies will often attempt to sell you large, splashy, and costly display ads. They look great and give your advertisement high visibility. They also put the most money into a newspaper or advertising agency's bank accounts. It's your money. It's your cost-to-hire ratio. Take time to be a discriminating buyer. Evaluate results and adjust your strategy accordingly.

▲ **Strategy 17:** Outplacement

Are you able to answer the following questions?

- What are the major (nationally recognized) outplacement firms?
- What are the respected national and local outplacement firms in your area?
- What type of talent do these firms typically represent?
- What are the specific guidelines that you would follow to get your company's open job requisitions in front of candidates represented by these firms?

I recommend that you take time to track down the answers. A great place to start is the Association of Career Firms International (ACF International) at http://www.aocfi.org. You may want to jump to ACF International's *Find-a-Firm* directory, located at http://www.aocfi.org/faf.html, to identify firms in your immediate area. Contact these firms. Discuss ways that you may partner with them to recruit appropriate professionals from their outplacement programs. Create win-win relationships between your company and outplacement firms.

Strategy 18: Career Fairs

I don't know about you, but when I hear the words *career fair* I envision standing at a booth amid an onslaught of humanity, handing out trinkets, sucking on throat lozenges, and walking away with a mountain of résumés and, generally, very few viable leads at the end of a long day. Once again, career fairs are part of "the way we've always done things." I'm not saying that career fairs don't have their place. I'm just saying that those who are on the narrow road to recruiting excellence need to be very picky about how, when, and where to invest their time, energy, and dollars. When it comes to career fair participation:

- Pick and choose carefully based on demographics, past success, advertisement support, location, and other considerations. There are plenty of career fairs vying for your business. You can afford to be (and should be) very picky.

- Do it right, or don't do it at all. Don't you just hate it when your team is stuck at a dinky table handing out logo-embossed pencils while your competitor has set up a truly impressive booth (imagine pyrotechnics, cool interactive audiovisual, and a drawing to win a $2,000 laptop)? Budget constraints and cost/benefit analysis should guide your decision regarding whether to attend any given career fair. They will also influence your decisions concerning display and collateral-material expenditures. Still, you should seriously consider forgoing a career fair rather than embarrassing yourself and your company with an amateur or half-hearted presence.

- Perform a critical evaluation. Do the anticipated number of hires justify the expense? If you believe the expense is justified, remember to verify your belief by way of an objective post–career fair cost/benefit analysis.

- Is there a better use of your time, energy, and money than this career fair? Ask yourself this question and be honest when responding. If you cannot think of a more creative, more effective, less costly way to spend your day and your dollars, go ahead and break out the logo pencils and lozenges! Excellence is judged by *results.*

▲ Strategy 19: Government Resources

Local, state, and federal government agencies should be enlisted as part of your arsenal of sourcing-related resources. At no cost to you, government agencies will typically post open requisitions, screen applicants, and even arrange interviews when asked. I'm surprised by how underutilized these services are.

Most employers don't believe they will find their next employee standing in the unemployment line. Likewise, most folks standing in that line don't believe they'll find their next employer there. I believe there is a psychological stigma associated with government agencies such as the Unemployment Bureau, Welfare-to-Work program, and the like. The unspoken assumption is that only losers participate in these programs. I suggest to you that this is not the case.

I invite you to check things out for yourself and draw your own conclusions. Only you can determine what sourcing techniques work best for you. The point is to experiment with new and different sourcing methods.

Call your local library and ask to speak with the reference librarian. He or she can help you find contact information for appropriate government agencies. As a backup, contact your local chamber of commerce or the mayor's office for information concerning local agencies. Contact the governor's office or your local state representative's office for a list of state agencies. Contact your congressional representative's office or your senators' offices if you need assistance in finding federal agencies.

Remain open-minded. Be creative. Avoid ruts and keep your edge.

▲ **Strategy 20:** Social Services

Many social service and private nonprofit agencies in your area specialize in employment-related programs. Once again, your local reference librarian can point you in the right direction.

- What programs exist in your area?
- How might you partner with them to ensure that your company is taking advantage of the services?

An excellent example of these services is the Lincoln Training Center of South El Monte, California. Lincoln Training Center specializes in helping individuals with developmental disabilities find competitive employment. It also provides disabled employees with ongoing support services. Lincoln Training Center provides grounds keeping, custodial, retail assistance, and food services. Contact Lincoln Training Center at:

Lincoln Training Center
Attn: Vice President of Rehabilitation
2643 Loma Avenue
South El Monte, CA 91733
Telephone: (626) 442-0621 or (800) 949-4582
Fax: (626) 442-0177
E-mail: ltcmain@lincolntc.org
Website: http://www.lincolntc.org

Take advantage of such services offered in you area.

▲ **Strategy 21:** Professional Journals and Magazines

As part of our ongoing efforts to crawl into our clients' worlds, we have discussed the importance of asking clients to point us in the direction of the magazines and professional journals that are specific to their particular area of expertise. Every profession has magazines/journals that reach its particular niche audience:

- IT professionals often read magazines such as *Computerworld, InfoWorld, eWEEK, Wired,* and *CIO.*
- CPAs may subscribe to *Accounting Today* or *Practical Accountant.*
- Legal staff may read the *ABA Journal* or *Legal Affairs* magazine.

If your IT group opens a new requisition for a senior Oracle database administrator, you may wish to consider placing an advertisement in *Oracle Magazine* or *Oracle Internals* rather than (or in addition to) your local Sunday newspaper.

Many professional journals and magazines have classified advertising sections. Many rent their lists of subscribers or offer direct mail services. Publisher contact information is generally found within the first two or three pages of journals and magazines. Contact the publisher or sales department to request a media kit. The media kit will provide you with details regarding reader demographics, editorial focus, advertising options, and pricing. Similar information is also available through the Standard Rate and Data Service (SRDS) via the *Business Publication Advertising Source.* Your favorite advertising agency or the local library may have a copy that you can borrow. You can also subscribe to this comprehensive guide via the SRDS website at http://www.srds.com.

Recruiters rarely advertise within professional publications on a routine basis. Often the prices are prohibitive. Regardless of budgetary constraints, there is no reason why you cannot read these magazines and journals to gain insight into your client's world. The articles, editorial content, and advertisements are full of company and individual names. The savvy recruiter will utilize this source of networking and direct recruiting information.

This is one of the many sourcing techniques that third-party recruiters use to track down the tough-to-find candidates that Sunday classified advertisements fail to attract.

Let this technique from the headhunters' playbook work for you.

▲ **Strategy 22:** Associations

Most professions have dedicated professional associations. HR professionals often belong to organizations such as the Society of Human Resources Management (SHRM) and the American Society for Training and Development (ASTD). I recommend a visit to their respective websites at http://www.shrm.org and http://www.astd.org.

If you are searching for an individual within the equipment leasing field (sales, credit, equity, operations, trading, and other personnel), the Equipment Lessor Association (ELA) at http://www.elaonline.org is a great place for you to begin your search. If you need to hire a legal secretary, you may wish to contact Legal Secretaries International, Inc., at http://www.legalsecretaries.org.

For each of your open requisitions, you will most likely find one or more associations serving the specific professionals you seek. Logically, therefore, you may want to utilize associations as potential networking, advertising, and/or direct sourcing vehicles. Associations are information clearinghouses for their particular professions. As such, they can also help you further your general understanding of your clients' worlds.

Type the name of the profession and the word *association* into your favorite search engine or contact the reference librarian at your local library for assistance. The appropriate association is generally easy to find and immensely useful.

When you are involved in a technical recruiting assignment, it is helpful to remember that most technologies have their own user groups. These are associations of IT professionals who meet on a regular basis to further their understanding of the specific software they have in common. User groups are often established by the software manufacturer. They are typically national in scope with local chapters in most major metropolitan areas. They often hold an annual national user group conference and sponsor a variety of local, regional, and national seminars and workshops throughout the year. When stymied by a tough-to-fill technical search (SAP, PeopleSoft, Oracle, Lawson, whatever), user groups can be your ticket to the inside track. Type the name of the technology and the words *user group* into your favorite search engine—for example, "Lotus Notes User Group"—and enjoy this goldmine.

Don't forget about Internet newsgroups and listservs as well. Visit your favorite search engine and type the name of the particular skill you are looking for with the word *newsgroup* or *list* next to it—for example, "Oracle newsgroup" or "Oracle list." **Note:** Remember to bracket the words in quotation marks to narrow the number of results.

Subscribing to newsgroups and lists will give you instant access to the world's leading experts in virtually any technology. However, a word of caution is in order here. Etiquette (or "netiquette" as the case may be) dictates that we respect the fact that members belonging to professional associations, newsgroups, and lists do not want to be assaulted by recruiters. They belong to these organizations and groups to communicate with one another regarding areas of common interest and concern. Visiting an association meeting or seminar and accosting people with a recruiting pitch is generally not appreciated. Help-wanted postings to newsgroups and lists are often considered spam—that is, junk e-mail. You may be booted out of newsgroups or receive hate e-mail from other group members. Be thoughtful and discreet and ask group leaders or moderators for guidance as to how you might best approach their audience with employment-related information.

I would like to illustrate the value of these particular techniques with a personal success story: I enjoyed considerable success as an international recruiter of technical talent back in the early 1990s. The Internet was text-based at the time (that is, no browsers or graphics). I used a Lynx browser with a 2400-baud modem and a 386 computer to connect to a truly global community of technology experts through newsgroups and lists. I also personally attended Lotus Notes, Oracle, PowerBuilder, and other user-group meetings, seminars, workshops, and conferences on a regular basis. By way of this access to the inner circle of the world's leading technology experts, I was often able to fill requisitions before the ink had dried on the ineffective advertisements that my competitors ran in Sunday's classified section.

Crawling into your clients' worlds entails thinking like they think, reading what they read, participating in the associations and workshops, seminars, and conferences that they participate in. I liken the recruiter's world to that of a big-game hunter. If you are hunting lion, you had best learn to think like a lion:

- Where will it seek food, water, and shelter?
- What climate and geography would you typically find lions in?
- What are its habits and regular haunts?
- When does a lion eat, sleep, and hunt?
- Would you hunt lions during the day or are they nocturnal creatures?

Learn to think like the professionals you hope to recruit. Success is in the details!

▲ **Strategy 23:** Community Resources

Communities have a wide variety of untapped recruiting resources. Local communities typically have community newspapers, and local radio and television stations. They also have amateur theater, community orchestras, county fairs, and Fourth of July celebrations. Communities have churches and synagogues, a chamber of commerce, Rotary Club, the American Legion, the Newcomers Club, Welcome Wagon, and the list goes on. Each community high school typically has its own newspaper. High schools also have printed programs for every sporting event, concert, and theatrical presentation at their school.

- Build a high-visibility presence throughout the local community.

- Run an advertisement in the high school's football season program.

- Place a "we're hiring" message for newcomers though Welcome Wagon.

- Place a help-wanted note on church/synagogue bulletin boards.

- Place inexpensive ads in community newspaper, radio, and TV media.

- Sponsor a summer intern program for local high school and college students.

- Make personal guest appearances on local radio and TV programs.

- Sponsor a recruiting booth at the county fair.

Be creative! Experiment with new ideas and analyze the results to determine what sourcing methods work best for you. Low-cost investments will often yield impressive dividends!

▲ **Strategy 24:** Employee Referrals

A thoughtfully conceived and well-implemented employee referral program is an essential ingredient in the recipe for building an excellent recruitment program.

Employees are the lifeblood of every organization. They have a stake in the continued success of their organization. They are in contact with family, friends, acquaintances, and competitors throughout the larger community. They know what it takes to fit in and succeed at your particular company. Logically, therefore, your employees can be a powerful recruiting source. A well-run employee referral program will:

- Offer clear and concise instructions
- Time-stamp every submission to avoid duplication and confusion
- Follow-up with a thank-you and candidate contact
- Maintain a meticulously organized referral tracking system
- Offer incentives (recognition and reward)
- Tie incentives to a clearly defined retention period
- Use creative ideas to keep the program exciting

Clear and concise instructions encourage participation while avoiding confusion. Make sure employees understand all submission guidelines (résumé format, when, where, and to whom submissions may be made) and anticipated outcomes such as:

- "We will acknowledge receipt of all referrals with forty-eight business hours."

- "We will make initial contact with every referral within five business days."
- "We will notify you of any/all referral-hires within forty-eight hours of offer acceptance."
- "You will receive $2,500 (minus applicable taxes and withholding) on the payday immediately following your referral's successful completion of ninety days of employment with our company."

Employees often refer personal friends. Your employees will feel justifiably upset if you drop the ball and fail to follow up on their referrals. I have seen poor follow-up turn a well-intentioned referral program into an employee relations nightmare! Keep things simple, well organized, and well executed. Be creative and add new prizes and other forms of recognition such as plaques, letters of recognition, gift certificates, extra vacation days, and special cash incentives for tough-to-fill requisitions. Whatever else you do with your employee referral program, remember to follow up.

▲ **Strategy 25:** Company Alumni

Remember the Big 8? Perhaps this was before your time. How about the Big 6? These days they are called the Big 4. Perhaps, one day, we'll have the Big ONE! The top accounting firms in the United States have done an excellent job over the years of enlisting their alumni as a marketing and recruiting army. Corporate recruiting would be well served by this particular page from the Big 4 playbook. Too often corporations are remiss in their efforts to stay in touch with former employees. This may be understandable when employees have left on bad terms. Then again, many employees leave on excellent terms and they would be happy to refer candidates to their former employer. We can do a better job of utilizing this resource by using the following:

• *Exit Interviews.* Most companies are not especially diligent when it comes to routine administration of formal exit interviews. This is unfortunate in that a rare opportunity for candid input is missed. The exit interview is also a natural time and place for an HR or recruiting representative to inquire: "May we contact you for employment referrals in the future?"

• *Alumni Newsletter.* It's easy and inexpensive to throw an online quarterly *Alumni Newsletter* together. It's a great way to stay in touch with old friends, improve public relations, and broaden your personal network of contacts. There are no mailing costs and it's a great place to post open requisitions and request alumni assistance.

• *Formal Alumni Referral Program.* Structure and administer this as you would your employee referral program. It's a very smart and cost-effective source of candidate referrals.

Remember, your company invested considerable time, effort, and money in each and every one of your former employees. Too often, we let that investment walk out the door with every resignation, termination, and retirement. Take time to develop your personal approach to alumni networking.

▲ Strategy 26: College and University Recruiting

As is true of career fairs in general, campus recruiting typically entails long days of table or booth sitting. We greet each student with a smile, a handshake, our latest and greatest "why you should work for us" brochure and a trinket or two. We walk away with a large stack of résumés that are often placed in some forgotten corner of the office where they collect dust. Certainly, there are those organizations that do an excellent job of sorting and cataloging each résumé received. They dutifully respond to each student with a thank-you note and a voluntary equal employment opportunity (EEO) questionnaire. I applaud these organizations for the courtesy and respect they show each applicant. However, this is a rarity.

The typical college or university recruiting staff travels from one campus career day to the next on autopilot. They rarely question whether campus career days yield sufficient numbers of viable candidates to warrant the continued investment of their recruiting time, energy, and dollars. Were this question to be honestly addressed, I believe that answer would be a resounding "No way!" Why, then, do so many recruiting departments continue down this path?

Members of the senior management team tend to have soft spots in their hearts for their alma maters. They take great pride in supporting the next generation of graduates from the "old school." As such, campus career days may endear recruiters to senior management while facilitating positive public relations. More often than not, recruiters attend campus career days simply because "it's the way we've always done things."

I believe college and university recruiting is in desperate need of revitalization. I urge you to thoughtfully and creatively consider the following question: Is there a better way to recruit young talent? I believe there is. I don't really need (or want) to meet hundreds or thousands of students. Ideally, I want to meet with those few who meet the specific criteria my company is looking for. Rather than spending a day meeting hundreds of random students, perhaps I could meet with key staff from the campus career planning and placement office. I could offer to fully partner with them toward hiring more of their graduates. After all, like me, they must ultimately define success in terms of the number of actual hires made. Who cares how many brochures and Frisbees have been handed out? Let's form a close working relationship to drive more hiring. I could offer to send them appropriate requisitions on a daily or weekly basis via fax or e-mail. I could instruct my recruiters to work closely with career planning and placement personnel to ensure that they have an adequate understanding of each position. I could ask them to screen student and alumni résumés for potential fits. I'd promise a personal phone or face-to-face interview for every qualified applicant they introduce to me. I could model our relationship along the lines of those I have with third-party recruiting vendors. Perhaps I could even pay a reasonable referral fee to the college or university for every hire made via their efforts on my behalf.

Can you imagine the delight of college or university officials who learn that their career planning and placement office is suddenly turning a profit! It could revolutionize campus recruiting and career planning and placement services.

Meet with key faculty, staff, and student leadership. These people have a vested interest in seeing their graduates land gainful employment. They also have a better lay-of-the-land regarding their student and graduate population than I do. I could ask them questions such as:

- "What student organizations on campus might I contact?"
- "Does the campus newspaper accept employment advertisements?"
- "Are there opportunities to guest-lecture, present seminars, or workshops?"
- "If you were trying to recruit the best and brightest graduates, how would you go about it?"

Remember, recruiting is an art, not a science. Take time to rethink and revitalize your approach to college and university recruiting. Have fun, explore, try new approaches, and review them with a critical eye.

▲ **Strategy 27:** Alumni Associations

Alumni have a vested interest in the placement of graduates from their alma mater. Emotionally they want to support the college or university from which they graduated. Practically speaking, their own degrees mean more when their alma mater is respected as a school with highly desirable (marketable) graduates.

Recruiters generally overlook alumni associations. I recommend contacting alumni association officers to brainstorm regarding potential avenues of partnership. Perhaps you could offer to:

- Run an advertisement within the alumni newsletter.

- Network with alumni to fill key positions within your company. For example, work with the alumni office to identify MBA graduates, CPAs, attorneys, and so forth. These niche alumni groups could be called on whenever you have an open requisition specific to their field. Contact could be via telephone, e-mail, fax, or snail mail as per individual alumnus preference.

- Establish a formal alumni referral program. Offer to make a cash donation to their school (or to the association itself) for every placement via their efforts on your behalf.

- Offer to make a cash donation in return for a direct-mail survey to designated alumni. For example, I think it would be fascinating to survey graduates from top MBA programs regarding their insights into how to best recruit MBAs. Do you suppose nursing school graduates just might have meaningful suggestions regarding how to best recruit RNs and LPNs?

Be creative. Alumni associations are easy to locate and approach. Employees at your own company can help you open doors to the alumni associations to which they belong. Some associations will be more receptive than others. As always, you'll want to creatively experiment and critically evaluate the results. Will this work for you? You'll never know unless you try.

▲ **Strategy 28:** Nontraditional Schools and Programs

Everything we've considered regarding college and university and alumni association resources may also be applied to the wide variety of nontraditional schools and educational programs. Take time to think about how you might best take advantage of the following programs.

Technical Institutes

ITT Technical Institute and Devry Institute come to mind. Check them out at http://www2.itt-tech.edu and http://www.devry.edu/ respectively. ITT Technical Institute serves more than thirty thousand students through its eighty sites in thirty states. It offers associate and bachelor degree programs designed to prepare students for careers in fields such as computer networking, computer drafting and design, automated manufacturing, electronics, and telecommunications, among others.

Devry has more than seventy-five campuses throughout the United States and Canada. The institute offers programs in information technology, technical and telecommunications management, accounting, business, computers, and electronics. Having merged with Keller Graduate School of Management in 1987, Devry now offers master degree programs in business administration, business administration/educational management, accounting and financial management, human resource management, information systems management, project management, public administration, and telecommunications management. In 1996, Devry joined forces with Becker CPA Review and subsequently with Conviser Duffy CPA Review. Via Becker-Conviser, Devry now offers preparation courses for state-administered certified public accountant, certified management accountant, and chartered financial analyst exams at more than two hundred locations.

Continuing Education Programs

Local high schools, YMCAs, YWCAs, community colleges, traditional colleges and universities, among others, offer continuing education programs covering a wide variety of topics. Take time to investigate these offerings in your community. Contact appropriate staff to explore recruiting-related synergies.

Certification Preparation Programs

If you can think of a certification exam, chances are there is a program (through school, workshop, or seminar) to help students prepare for it. Typing the words *"exam preparation"* (in quotations) in Yahoo's search engine yields about 1,340,000 hits. You can narrow the field by keying the type of examination outside of the quotation marks as follows:

"Exam Preparation" NASD—This narrows the hits from 1,340,000 to 3,770. Additional keywords may be utilized to further narrow the number of responses.

"Exam Preparation" NASD Ohio—This brings the number of hits to a more manageable 319. Not every hit is applicable. American Education Systems, http://www.amedsys.com, and the American Institute of Banking, http://www.aba.com, are among the relevant hits offering examination preparation courses for NASD certification.

Play with different keyword combinations to zero in on your search target:

"Exam Preparation" CPA—This yields 26,100 hits.

"Exam Preparation" CPA California—Adding the word
California narrows the field to 2,200 hits.

"Exam Preparation" CPA California Sacramento—This drops
the hits down to 220.

Note: Many Internet users become discouraged when their
search engine queries yield unmanageable numbers of hits. *Use
of quotation marks* coupled with *experimentation with various additional keywords* is critical to effective Internet search engine utilization. I cannot overemphasize the importance of utilizing
quotation marks to bracket your central concept. For example,
look what happens when I type in the exact same combination of
keywords without quotation marks:

Exam Preparation CPA California Sacramento—My number of
hits jumps from 220 to 1,650! Why? In the former example, I am
asking Yahoo to search for sites that contain the concept *exam
preparation.* In the latter example, I am requesting any/all sites that
contain the word *exam* and the word *preparation.*

Remember that typing *recruiting excellence* yields 2,200,000
hits. Add quotation marks to make it "recruiting excellence" and
the number of hits drops to 2,410, which is about one-tenth of 1
percent of 2,200,000 (.11 to be exact).

Apply expertise and creativity to place your recruiting team
in that top 1 percent.

▲ Strategy 29: Military Outplacement

Each year, thousands upon thousands of experienced professionals are separated from active duty in the United States Armed Forces. Doctors, nurses and medical assistants, administrative personnel, logistics experts, programmer/analysts, and database administrators are among them. Literally hundreds of professions are represented.

The 1991 Defense Authorization Act (Public Law 101-510) required the office of the Secretary of Defense to provide employment assistance to separating military service personnel and their spouses. Operation Transition and the Defense Outplacement Referral System (DORS) were born. In recent years, the Department of Defense has renamed the DORS program to Job Search and linked it with the Department of Labor's America's Job Bank.

Job Search offers a unique, no-cost résumé registry and referral system. You must register to participate in this program at http://dod.jobsearch.org/register. You will be asked to provide information such as:

- Your organization's name
- Your telephone number
- Your fax number
- The name of the person in your organization that Job Search personnel may contact to request additional information concerning your organization as needed

The registration process is quick and easy. The system is very user-friendly and the turnaround time is enviable. Over the years, I have hired a number of candidates by way of the DORS (now Job Search) program. In all likelihood, I would not have found these individuals otherwise.

The program is not without its flaws. For example, I have sometimes found contact information to be outdated or inaccurate. In such instances, I have had difficulty getting in touch with the candidates. Despite its flaws, I am grateful that the program is available. It is clearly a worthwhile source to have in your sourcing tool kit.

▲ **Strategy 30:** Research Firms

Research is a cornerstone of effective recruiting. Requisition requirements are utilized as the road map by which we target prospective candidates.

When your recruiting department is understaffed or operating under budgetary constraints, utilization of an outside research firm can provide valuable and cost-effective support. They are also especially useful in putting out direct-recruiting feelers into competitive companies when your organization prefers to keep its own hands clean regarding such practices.

Research is a competitive market and there are plenty of firms from which to choose. Generally, research firms charge by the hour. Fees of $100 per hour and higher are not unusual. Still, effective utilization of a research firm will typically yield viable candidates at a fraction of the price of outside recruiting firm support.

Although on the expensive end of the fee spectrum, I consider Workstream (formerly OmniPartners) among the best in the business. Workstream, Inc., will locate appropriate individuals for your open requisitions and prescreen them for you according to your exact specifications. You may readily find better prices than those offered by Workstream. In my opinion, the quality of Workstream's work justifies its price. Check the firm out at http://www.workstreaminc.com or toll-fee 1-866-470-WORK (9675).

Utilize your favorite search engine to identify alternative recruiting research firms in your area by entering the parameters of "recruiting research firms" or "recruiting research services"

You may also wish to check out a short and well-written article entitled "Getting the Most out of Recruiting Research Firms" by Christine Hirsh of Chicago Resources Corporation (http://www.chicagoresources.com). You may locate this article at: http://www.recruitersworld.com/articles/rw/christine/research1.asp.

▲ **Strategy 31:** Contingency Recruiters

Recruiting is a multibillion-dollar industry. Contingency recruiters earn their fair share of these revenues by consistently delivering results where internal recruiters have failed.

You've got to love contingency recruiting. Contingency recruiters are the guerilla fighters of the recruiting world. Unlike in-house recruiters or retained search consultants, contingency recruiters don't earn a dime unless they deliver the goods. When your next paycheck is contingent on the next search you bring to fruition (that is, a hiring decision), you become very adept at sourcing, recruiting, and closing recruiting assignments. If you don't become very good very quickly, you don't tend to survive in the industry.

In Chapter 1, I discussed my recommendations for how to structure optimal vendor agreements. I will avoid repeating myself here. As a *sourcing* technique, contingency recruiting should be considered a most viable option. When your only financial obligation is tied to successful results, you have no downside. In fairness to all concerned, I suggest you avoid recruiting vendors altogether (contingency and retained) unless you are fully prepared to do the following:

- Invest whatever time and effort necessary to communicate openly and honestly with the outside recruiter regarding your requisition, your company, and your hiring process.

- Provide the vendor with regular updates and timely feedback. Show respect for the time and effort invested on your behalf via prompt and courteous follow-up.

- Pay your invoice in a timely manner.

- Reward excellent service with future business when appropriate.

Contingency recruiting free-for-all is a common mistake made by corporate recruiting departments. It stems from the misconception that recruiters should send open requisitions to as many firms as possible and let them fight it out on the streets. Whoever contacts the best candidate in the fastest time wins. The result is generally a mad dash to get in touch with a limited number of viable candidates in a specific market. The candidates are often annoyed by multiple recruiter contacts (this in turn may damage your company's reputation), and the best recruiters quickly conclude that your requisitions are a waste of their time and effort. The odds for success are better when recruiters invest their time and effort on behalf of companies that they can really partner with. This said, I suggest you build partnerships with select recruiting-support vendors on mutually beneficial terms and conditions.

▲ **Strategy 32:** Retained Search

A retained search makes me think of a twenty-dollar hamburger. If you were in the mood for a world-class hamburger, why would you pay twenty dollars when an equally great five-dollar burger is available down the street? ***Note:*** For argument's sake, let's assume comparable quality of ground beef and bun, as well the cooks' culinary acumen.

There may be perfectly legitimate reasons for coughing up the extra fifteen bucks:

- Perhaps, the twenty-dollar burger is served at an elegant restaurant, while the five-dollar burger is served at a roadside diner. You prefer fine china, silverware, and world-class waiters to a stool at the counter.

- Perhaps you'd be just as happy in either locale. However, in that you are entertaining a senior management candidate the choice is obvious.

- Perhaps you've just won the lotto and you want to celebrate.

- Perhaps you are hoping to impress a date.

Again, I believe retained search is like the expensive burger. You pay more for the same meal but the fancy presentation and relational ambiance is something to behold. There are perfectly legitimate reasons for choosing to use a retained search. I've previously mentioned a few such reasons:

- You have an especially high-level search.

- You need to ensure the utmost confidentiality and tact.

- You believe you need the door-opening power of a high-visibility name.
- You may want to project a certain corporate image.

Given the choice, would you drive a Mercedes or a Volkswagen? Either car will get you where you're going. Sometimes, you may intentionally want to choose comfort and style over function. Personally, I'm convinced that a solid contingency firm can hold its own against the twenty-dollar burger guys any day of the week.

▲ **Strategy 33:** Open Houses and Other Planned Events

We've taken a look at typical sourcing events such as career fairs and campus career days. We should also note that an open house is another sourcing technique that is commonly put to good use. Several considerations are key to an effective event.

Have a Plan

Choose your date, time, and location carefully. Consider what you are hoping to accomplish, and then plan accordingly. Is this an informal "get to know us" event, or do you hope to have potential candidates fill out applications and spend one-on-one prescreening time with one of your recruiters? Will Wednesday evening's baseball game tie up traffic in your area? Will inclement weather be a potential factor this time of year? Will an after-hours open house need more food and catering support than an afternoon event? Should you line up a guest speaker or special presentation to attract more people? Would this help or detract from your recruiting message?

If held at your offices, will the open house be disruptive to other workers? If after hours, have you given adequate consideration to security issues regarding the safety of your visitors, staff, and company property? If held outside the office, what location is readily accessible to your target audience?

Provide Collateral Material

Especially when held off-site, be sure to have plenty of collateral material on hand to include an adequate supply of business cards, employment applications, brochures, giveaway trinkets, pens, pencils, paper, name tags, and so forth.

Have Refreshments on Hand

Have plenty of coffee, tea, soft drinks, water, and "nibble food" on hand. Take care that you also have an adequate supply of plates, cups, napkins, and utensils. Don't forget the sugar, cream, sugar and cream substitutes, salt and pepper, condiments, and trash receptacles. Better yet, do you know an inexpensive caterer?

Get the Word Out!

Run advertisements, hand out flyers, do a direct-mail piece, post invitations on the Internet (use newsgroups and lists when netiquette allows, which are free). Notify outplacement firms, career planning and placement offices, user groups, and professional associations by fax, telephone, e-mail, or formal invitation. Be creative.

Ensure Your Event Is Adequately Staffed

Be sure to have enough host personnel on hand to effectively handle visitor traffic flow. There is nothing worse than having your visitors milling around without a host representative to talk to. Ideally, you'll also want to avoid overstaffing an event. It is a waste of time and effort to have your staff milling about with no visitors to talk to. As you gain experience with event planning, you will begin to have a sense of how many staff to have on hand for specific types of events.

Follow Up

Be sure to have a plan in place regarding appropriate follow-up. Don't spoil a successful event with a disappearing act. This can be as simple as a postcard or e-mail stating: "Thank you for coming! We enjoyed meeting you and appreciate your interest in our company." **Note:** When a formal application has been received, additional formal follow-up steps should be taken. For example, send a voluntary EEO self-disclosure form.

Anticipate Other Contingencies

Open houses are one of many event options you will want to experiment with in determining what type of events work best for you. There are community, school, and association events in which you may wish to participate. There are local, regional, and national conventions; trade shows; county and state fairs; and more. You can sponsor sporting events, seminars, workshops, and TV or radio programs. The list is only as limited as your creativity. Success or failure of any given event will be largely determined by your attention to planning, execution, and follow-up (or the lack thereof).

As always, you should look at events in terms of their bottom-line results. Do the results justify the cost, time, effort, or money?

▲ **Strategy 34:** Competitors

Utilization of competitors as a recruiting source may be broken down into two distinct strategies: direct sourcing and peer networking.

Direct Sourcing

Direct sourcing is bread and butter to the third-party recruiting industry. On one hand, those of us in corporate recruiting are generally eager to hire individuals with experience relevant to our specific industry. On the other hand, we typically try to avoid earning a reputation for being raiders of our competition. Moreover, we certainly do not want our competition to respond in-kind by raiding our personnel. We use outside research recruiting firms to do our dirty work for us and we pay them handsomely for their services. We also utilize classified advertising, open houses, and other reputation-safe sourcing methodologies to attract our competitors' personnel. All is fair in love and recruiting.

Peer Relationships and Alliances

Informal peer-to-peer alliances can be very useful. The third-party recruiting industry relies heavily on such alliances to drive *split business.* This is a cooperative effort between one agency with a job requisition and another agency that provides the candidate who is hired by the client. The two agencies split the fee. As a general rule, clients only interface with the agency to which the requisition was given. The client is often unaware that a "split" has taken place. Splitting business is a very common practice in the third-party recruiting industry. It can only help us, the clients, in that more recruiting resources are engaged on our behalf without any additional investment of time, effort, or money. When handled properly, split business is seamless to the client.

Within the corporate recruiting world, recruiter-to-recruiter alliances need to follow certain guidelines. For example, confidential and proprietary information must not be shared. I may let a competitor know that I'm in the market for a few additional credit analysts and that I'd appreciate his or her referrals. I will not reveal that the positions are open because our director of credit just resigned and took four of our best analysts with her. I won't reveal the specific structure of the compensation and benefits associated with the position. I won't mention that the new analysts are being hired in anticipation of increased sales activity due to the upcoming launch of a new product offering. In other words, I won't compromise my company's interests.

Caution should be exercised. Still, peer-to-peer relationships can be an excellent source of information. You can talk shop and pick up new ideas, such as:

- Maybe your peer is willing to tell you about the successful open house she just held and share ideas that will help you with your next event.

- Maybe her company recently hired one credit analyst and she would be happy to pass your name and phone number on to a few of the runner-up candidates as a personal favor to you (and to them).

- Maybe she wants to enroll in an Internet recruiting workshop and wonders if you might be interested in joining her.

- Perhaps her company has just declared Chapter 11 and she has received a pink slip. Your relationship could position you to snatch up an experienced peer before other competitors even know she is available.

Relationships make the world go around. Whether through your local SHRM meetings, a recruiting seminar, HR conference, or introductory phone calls, take time to get to know your peers.

▲ **Strategy 35:** Networking

Speaking of relationships, an active and growing personal-contact network is invaluable in our profession (as it is in any profession, for that matter). Who are these contacts?

They are family, friends, coworkers, competitors, your neighbors, alumni, fellow church/club/association members, folks that you meet at a conference, PTA meeting, or the guy that sat next to you on a recent flight home. The difference between someone you know and a contact is that you have taken time to capture and catalogue information that will enable you to call on that individual at some future date to request or provide personal or professional assistance.

I may know Fred as someone I say hello to in church. He is someone I *know*. If I note that Fred is an immigration attorney with Dewey, Cheatem, and Howe and I ask him for a business card for my Rolodex file, he becomes a *contact*. When I am working on a search with possible immigration implications, perhaps I can send some business Fred's way. Perhaps my company will want to hire an in-house immigration expert someday. I'll call Fred for candidate leads.

The best relationships are give and take. If you formalize and organize your contact files with a Rolodex, excel spreadsheet, database, or good old-fashioned filing cabinet, you'll be glad you did. Over the years, I have contacted local, regional, and national officers of associations that are relevant to the searches I have worked on. In seeking their advice, I have asked: "If you were me, how would you go about finding someone with these credentials?"

I've also chatted with them to get the latest word on the

street: What is new in your profession these days? Who is hiring; who is cutting back? What ever happened to . . . ?

I have also expressed genuine interest in their lives: What is new with you lately? Last time we spoke you were expecting your third child. How was your vacation? Have you been out on the golf course lately? Is there anything I can do for you today?

It's a small world. International recruiting may play a significant role in our overall employment strategy. It is beyond the scope of this book for me to specify each available visa option. I would like to encourage you to become familiar with the variety of work visas that are available through the Bureau of Citizenship and Immigration Services at http://uscis.gov/graphics/formsfee/index .htm.

I find the ease of hiring Canadian and Mexican employees via the North American Free Trade Agreement (NAFTA) of particular interest. Notwithstanding certain restrictions, NAFTA allows Canadian or Mexican men and women to enter the United States on a temporary basis to engage in certain business activities (as specified in NAFTA's Schedule I) without additional employment authorization. There are nuances to NAFTA and you should involve legal counsel to ensure that you are in compliance.

Schedule I lists sixty-three types of professionals who may enter the United States to engage in employment activities pursuant to a contract or offer of employment, including the following:

• *General.* Accountant, architect, computer systems analyst, disaster relief insurance claims adjuster, economist, engineer, forester, graphic designer, hotel manager, industrial designer, interior designer, land surveyor, landscape architect, lawyer, librarian, management consultant, mathematician/statistician, range manager/range conservationist, research assistant, scientific technician/technologist, social worker, sylviculturist/forestry specialist, technical publications writer, urban planner/geographer, vocational counselor

- *Medical/Allied Professionals.* Dentist, dietitian, medical laboratory technologist, nutritionist, occupational therapist, pharmacist, physician (teaching or research only), physiotherapist/physical therapist, psychologist, recreational therapist, registered nurse, veterinarian

- *Scientists.* Agriculturist/agronomist, animal breeder, animal scientist, apiculturist, astronomer, biochemist, biologist, chemist, dairy scientist, entomologist, epidemiologist, geneticist, geochemist, geologist, geophysicist (oceanographer), horticulturist, meteorologist, pharmacologist, physicist, plant breeder, poultry scientist, soil scientist, zoologist

- *Teachers.* College, seminary, university

As you can see, this is a fairly diverse list. On any particular search, you may want to look north or south of the border for your next employee.

▲ **Strategy 37:** Internal Postings and Promotions

Recruiting professionals are tasked with sourcing the best available talent for each open requisition entrusted to us. Although we may influence a hiring manager's decision, we do not typically control that decision.

Recruitment does not occur in a vacuum. While working to attract new blood into our organizations, we must also take steps to ensure that we are taking care of our current employees. Employee relations' best practices encourage us to promote from within whenever possible. Internal promotions allow us to challenge, reward, and develop our best internal talent. As an added benefit, promotions often simplify our recruiting task. Backfilling a position vacated by a promotion is often easier than finding individuals with the higher level of experience and credentials required by the original requisition. When setting up an effective internal posting program, it is best to do the following:

• *Open internal postings before searching for external candidates.* For example, you may wish to post requisitions internally for one to two weeks prior to considering outside candidates.

• *Provide clear rules of consideration.* You may wish to specify that employees must have been in their current positions for at least one year prior to responding to an internal posting. Make sure that all employees have easy and equitable access to all postings. Make sure that the application process specifies when, how, and to whom employees may submit their applications.

- ***Follow up.*** It's bad enough when outside candidates fall through the cracks. Whenever we fail to adequately take care of our own, we invite an employee relations firestorm.

Excellence is a by-product of meticulous execution.

▲ **Strategy 38:** Candidate Pipeline

At last we come to the ever-popular candidate pipeline, which is a database of prescreened candidates that has been proactively created and maintained in anticipation of future hiring needs. The term *pipeline* comes from the concept of having viable candidates at each stage of the hiring process:

- Introduction
- Prescreen
- Interview
- Reference check
- Hire

Anytime a new requisition opens up, you simply tap the pipeline for your next hire. It's a great concept, in theory. Unfortunately, there is a fly in the ointment. The best candidates do not tend to be available for very long. When you've taken time to source, prescreen, and interview top-notch professionals, they will generally expect that you'll be making a hiring decision in the near future. They may become disillusioned with you and your company when asked to play a protracted waiting game.

Should you wish to start and maintain a viable pipeline, I suggest the following:

• *Set realistic candidate expectations.* Let your candidates know exactly what you are doing. Let them know that you are building a candidate pipeline composed of individuals that your company may have an interest hiring if or when appropriate requisitions open up. Let them know that you are interested in getting to know them better over time while they get to know you and your company.

• **_Keep management informed._** Management is often under the misconception that recruiters can keep large numbers of great candidates "warm" on the proverbial back burner. In my experience, hot talent has low tolerance for lukewarm status. When you find exceptional talent, keep management in the loop.

• **_Create a new job position._** Consider creating a position when necessary to take advantage of a great candidate.

• **_Don't overextend._** When attempting to keep hot candidates warm, you will greatly improve the likelihood of success when you maintain regular contact. There are only so many hours in each day. You will be hard-pressed to maintain a large pipeline of back-burner candidates while also working on your current front-burner requisitions. With this in mind, I believe your pipeline should generally have no more than a half-dozen candidates at any given time. More than this and you typically won't have enough hours in the day to nurture each relationship.

Huge pipelines are great, in theory. In reality, they are rarely manageable. Keep your pipeline small and a manageable. Anything else is a pipe dream.

▲ **Strategy 39:** Roadkill

Dell, K-Mart, Andersen Consulting, Enron, United Airlines, and other companies have displaced thousands of experienced professionals in recent years. Ups and downs in corporate fortunes will always generate a good number of employee terminations across the employment landscape. Human resources departments generally spearhead efforts to help displaced employees land on their feet. One company's loss is another's gain.

Next time you hear about a massive layoff, downsizing, or corporate collapse, call the human resources department of the hapless organization involved and offer to help them place appropriate people within your company.

Your phone call will typically be welcome. You may find a number of experienced and immediately available candidates who are eager to hear about opportunities with your company. The best sourcing techniques are win-win.

▲ **Strategy 40:** Brainstorm

As we've seen earlier, crawling into our clients' worlds may entail tracking down a professional association or the specific journals, newsgroups, and e-mail lists to which our target candidates subscribe. It may mean contacting alumni associations and attending trade shows or conferences. It is *always* an attempt to step into our candidates' shoes for a moment and think as they would think:

- If I were a CPA, what would be the best ways to get in touch with me?

- What journals would I read?

- What associations would I belong to?

- What seminars, workshops, and conferences might I attend?

The answers to questions such as these are as varied as the individuals within each profession. Our answers, and therefore our recruiting sourcing techniques, are restricted only by the limits of our creativity, time, energy, and resources.

I love to ask my recruiters the following question: "If every sourcing technique you know to try fails, how are you going to fill this position?" **Note:** There is only one answer: You'll have to think of a new sourcing technique.

Rent a billboard. Pay a pilot to pull a WE'RE HIRING! banner behind her airplane. Place ads on checkout bags at the grocery store. Rent a booth at the mall. Pay a Boy Scout troop to deliver flyers door-to-door (as a troop fund-raising effort). Hold a free résumé-writing seminar and present your sponsor sales pitch to the attendees.

Take inspiration from Thomas Edison's ten thousand attempts to make a lightbulb. And when all else fails, you'll have to think of a new sourcing technique.

CHAPTER 3

Diversity Recruitment

▲ **Strategy 41:** Attracting and Retaining Diverse Talent

You've got to love www.mapquest.com: plug in any zip code or city by name and, voila, a detailed map of the specified location appears on screen. We can select a second location and this on-line program will provide map- and text-based instructions regarding exactly how to travel from our point of origin to our point of destination. It's a marvel of modern technology. With a few clicks of the mouse, we are able to secure turn-by-turn instructions to virtually any street address. Likewise, were we able to map diversity recruitment strategies with similar ease we would want to visualize the following three things:

1. Our precise starting position

2. Our destination

3. The best route by which to complete our journey

It's a Twister!

As I reflect on these three aspects of this hypothetical road map, I am struck by the ironic nature of the starting position we so often find ourselves in. We are not born with fear or prejudice of one another. Having been socialized toward gradual abandonment of our gentler nature we desperately seek to regain it via codification (antidiscrimination law), lofty vision, and mission statements and how-to gurus du jour. Our quest is not unlike that of Dorothy Gale in the *Wizard of Oz.* Like Dorothy, we long to find our way back home—in this case, to the very characteristics of tolerance and inclusion we were born with and that have remained within us (albeit buried) all along.

Somewhere Over the Rainbow

The classic 1939 MGM film, *The Wizard of Oz,* begins with black-and-white footage of daily life in a dark and dreary Kansas dust-bowl community. We are introduced to Dorothy, a little girl who dreams of a land beyond her lackluster existence, one rich in color. Likewise, our quest toward diversity must begin with noticing our current condition. Our dissatisfaction with the way things are becomes fertile ground for dreams of what might be. Unfortunately, we may be all too comfortable with the way things are and have always been. We may be anesthetized to seeing our current situation with truly objective and inquisitive eyes.

I recently shared the following starting-point perspective with a fellow SHRM diversity committee members in an article I authored entitled "We Still Have A Long Way To Go": In 2004, 62,772 claims alleging discriminatory hiring and/or employment practices in violation of Title VII of the Civil Rights Act of 1964 were filed with the EEOC. That's one Title VII-related claim every 8.5 minutes of every hour of every day 365 days a year!

Organizations such as Fair Chance (http://www.fairchance .org) and the National Committee on Pay Equity (http://www .pay-equity.org) are dedicated to shedding light on the inequities behind such claims:

- Women earn approximately 77 cents for every dollar men earn.

- Latinas earn 56 cents for every dollar white men earn.

- African-American men earn 75 percent of what white males earn.

- White college graduates earned 11 percent more than Asian college graduates.

- Women with master's degrees average $4,765 less than men with bachelor's degrees.

The cost of settling and/or litigating 62,772 claims is astronomical. You may recall the single claim in which The United States Information Agency awarded approximately $533 million in damages and back pay to 1,134 women—the largest settlement to date of a federal sex discrimination case (March 2000). More recently, 1.6 million women have claimed that Wal-Mart has discriminated against them in both pay and promotions. Their class-action suit could easily dwarf the aforementioned $533 million settlement.

The hidden cost of discrimination is immeasurable. "If you have to walk [into work] in the morning and worry about the color of your skin, your accent, the fact that you are gay or lesbian, or what people are thinking, then all of your energy is not going to be directed toward your job."[1]

Compromised energy and focus yield compromised bottom-line results for U.S. business. The toll exacted on individuals is often overlooked. Discrimination wounds the human spirit. It creates an atmosphere of fear and mistrust that stresses mind and body. According to the Centers for Disease Control, the American Psychological Association and the National Institute for Occupational Safety and Health among others, stress is responsible for a more than $300 billion annual drain on corporate profits ($7,500 per employee) via:

- Decreased productivity and compromised quality
- Job burnout (thought to be as much as 40 percent of U.S. workers)
- Work-related accidents (safety) resulting in workers compensation claims
- Absenteeism and high employee turnover
- Memory loss, confused thinking, irrational decisions
- Heart disease, cancer, immune disorders, and obesity, among others

We have an uphill battle ahead of us to keep diversity recruitment and retention issues on executive management's front burners. Toward encouraging buy-in, we frequently engage in complex and expensive surveys and analysis. In my experience, these activities generally produce more rhetoric than action. We delay actually doing something about diversity for the sake of talking about it. Our formal efforts to build a business case can turn into a rather circuitous detour from the common sense conclusions that are readily apparent (here and now) when we simply focus on our honest, gut responses to a handful of straightforward questions:

- Does my company appear to provide equal opportunity regardless of sex, age, religion, sexual preference, disabilities, and so forth?

- Are women and men equally represented in management?

- Are minorities fairly represented?

- Are folks paid equally for comparable duties?

- Are people truly given equal access and opportunity for hire, education, advancement?

Although there may be diversity and equal treatment "somewhere over the rainbow," we know intuitively that it does not exist in most human enterprises. Thus, we begin with an honest assessment of our starting point and a vision of where we hope to arrive.

At the risk of sounding overly touchy-feely and simplistic, I suggest we think of our desired destination as a time and place where we may honestly answer yes to questions regarding issues of diversity (fairness, equality, inclusion, etc):

- Yes, we have equal employment opportunity for all.

- Yes, we respect and treat all people fairly.

- Yes, we have open and honest communication.

- Yes, we include everyone in processes to promote and protect diversity.

In other words, we need a vision with gut appeal. It must have buy-in at a simple, emotional, "I get it" level. It must be accessible (known, understood, and believed) by all who are expected to participate in truly meaningful ways to achieve it.

We're Not in Kansas Anymore

While envisioning our destination, we may be painfully aware of our present organizational shortcomings. Having removed any rose-colored glasses by which we maintained entrenched patterns of organizational behavior, we may have a rather disconcerting feeling that "we're not in Kansas anymore!"

Yesterday we assured ourselves that "we don't have a diversity problem here. While it is true that we do not have any minorities in management, we are not prejudiced. We simply have not been able to find candidates of color with the necessary credentials." The realization that we are no longer in Kansas begins with an honest appraisal of the situation. No longer comfortable with what we see, we are less able to tolerate a head-in-the-sand approach to diversity. We see the situation simply as it is—without excuse or candy coating. We find ourselves making simple statements of fact, such as the following:

- Every member of our executive management team is a white male.

- Only 3 percent of our mid-level managers are female.

- We have no minorities in management.

- One percent of our employees are African American.

- Two percent of our employees are Latino.

- We have no disabled employees at this time.

- Ninety-five percent of the 1,000 employees we laid off last year were over the age of forty.

- Men received an average raise of 5 percent last year; Women averaged 3.5 percent raises.

In other words, we pull off defensive blinders and nail down the hard facts. With each apparent inequity or oddity we ask, "Why is this?"

Our quest for sound diversity recruitment practices must begin with the courage to intentionally see beyond our own private Kansas. We compare our gut-take on the situation with the facts as we are able to gather them. We enlist the aid of the Society for Human Resource Management (SHRM); local, state, and federal resources such as the mayor's office; the state unemployment bureau; and the Department of Labor to gather demographic data by which to compare our internal demographics. We begin to answer the question, "What *should* we look like given the realistic resources and talent available to us?"

Follow the Yellow Brick Road

The yellow brick road had many twists and turns. Obstacles to success included dark forests, enchanted fields, and determined adversaries. Despite its challenges, it was nonetheless a proven route to the destination sought by those with the courage and conviction to make the journey. I believe the road to optimal diversity recruitment is paved with common sense. Do you *really* want to recruit young African-American graduates? Forget about running a help-wanted ad in your newspaper or recruitment website. Pick up the phone and contact the career planning and placement offices of the following thirty-nine United Negro College Fund (UNCF) colleges:

Allen University, Columbia, SC http://www.allenuniversity.edu/

Benedict College, Columbia, SC http://www.benedict.edu/

Bennett College, Greensboro, NC http://www.bennett.edu/

Bethune-Cookman College, Daytona Beach, FL http://www.bethune.cookman.edu/

Claflin University, Orangeburg, SC http://www.claflin.edu/

Clark Atlanta University, Atlanta, GA http://www.cau.edu/

Dillard University, New Orleans, LA http://www.dillard.edu/

Edward Waters College, Jacksonville, FL http://www.ewc.edu/

Fisk University, Nashville, TN http://www.fisk.edu/

Florida Memorial University, Miami, FL http://www.fmuniv.edu/

Huston-Tillotson University, Austin, TX http://www.htu.edu/

Interdenominational Theological Center, Atlanta, GA http://www.itc.edu/

Jarvis Christian College, Hawkins, TX http://www.jarvis.edu/

Johnson C. Smith University, Charlotte, NC http://www.jcsu.edu/

Lane College, Jackson, TN http://www.lanecollege.edu/

LeMoyne-Owen College, Memphis, TN http://www.loc.edu/

Livingstone College, Salisbury, NC http://www.livingstone.edu/

Miles College, Birmingham, AL http://www.miles.edu/

Morehouse College, Atlanta, GA http://www.morehouse.edu/

Morris College, Sumter, SC http://www.morris.edu

Oakwood College, Huntsville, AL http://www.oakwood.edu/

Paine College, Augusta, GA http://www.paine.edu/

Paul Quinn College, Dallas, TX http://www.pqc.edu/

Philander Smith College, Little Rock, AR http://www.philander.edu/

Rust College, Holly Springs, MS http://www.rustcollege.edu/

Saint Augustine's College, Raleigh, NC http://www.st-aug.edu/

Saint Paul's College, Lawrenceville, VA http://www.saintpauls.edu/

Shaw University, Raleigh, NC http://www.shawuniversity.edu/

Spelman College, Atlanta, GA http://www.spelman.edu/

Stillman College, Tuscaloosa, AL http://www.stillman.edu/

Talladega College, Talladega, AL http://www.talladega.edu/

Texas College, Tyler, TX http://www.texascollege.edu/

Tougaloo College, Tougaloo, MS http://www.tougaloo.edu/

Tuskegee University, Tuskegee, AL http://www.tuskegee.edu/

Virginia Union University, Richmond, VA http://www.vuu.edu/

Voorhees College, Denmark, SC http://www.voorhees.edu/

Wilberforce University, Wilberforce, OH http://www.wilberforce.edu/

Wiley College, Marshall, TX http://www.wileyc.edu/

Xavier University, New Orleans, LA http://www.xula.edu/

Contact officers of any of the following African-American associations and organizations. Ask *their* advice regarding how to best attract (and retain) African-American talent:

African-American Associations and Organizations

National Urban League http://www.nul.org/

National Association for the Advancement of Colored People http://www.naacp.org/

United Negro College Fund http://www.uncf.org/

Association of African-American Web Developers http://www.aaawd.net/

National Black MBA Association http://www.nbmbaa.org/

National Society of Black Engineers http://www.nsbe.org/

Do you want to attract and retain Hispanics and Latinos? Contact representatives of professional organizations and associations created to serve this constituency:

Hispanic and Latino Associations

LatPro.com http://www.latpro.com/

Hispanic Business Women's Alliance http://www.hbwa.net/

Latin Business Association http://www.lbausa.com/

National Association of Hispanic Nurses http://www.thehispanicnurses.org/

National Society for Hispanic Professionals http://www.nshp.org/

National Society of Hispanic MBAs http://www.nshmba.org/

Need to increase your sensitivity and effectiveness in recruitment and retention issues specific to the disabled, gays, older workers, or veterans? Use common sense to seek out the organizations that serve these specific individuals.

Disability-Related Associations

National Federation of the Blind http://www.nfb.org/

National Association of the Deaf http://www.nad.org/

World Association of Persons with Disabilities http://www.wapd.org/

Disabled American Veterans National Headquarters http://www.dav.org/

National Association for Retarded Citizens (ARC) http://www.thearc.org

The Association for Persons with Severe Handicaps http://www.tash.org/

Sexual-Orientation Organizations

Gay Work (partnered with Monster.com) http://www.gaywork.com/

Center for Gender Sanity http://www.gendersanity.com/

Gay & Lesbian Medical Association http://www.glma.org/

Gay & Lesbian Alliance Against Defamation http://www.glaad.org/

International Foundation for Gender Education http://www.ifge.org/

Bisexual Resource Center http://www.biresource.org/

Miscellaneous

AARP http://www.aarp.org (for mature Americans)

Department of Veteran Affairs: http://www.va.gov

American Association for Affirmative Action http://www.affirmativeaction.org/

Society for Human Resource Management http://www.shrm.org

Rather than talking about our good intentions, let's roll up our sleeves and take simple, practical steps. Let's engage in dialogue with the very people we hope to attract. We will find them in the schools, associations, organizations, events, and publications to which they voluntarily belong. Once we have established links with diverse communities, we must ask intelligent questions, such as:

- What must we do to be most effective in our efforts to attract more professional women (Blacks, Latinos, etc.) into our organization?
- What issues of the Black community must we be sensitive toward to create a welcoming and inclusive workplace?
- How do we help gays feel welcome and accepted?

Each group will have specific insights to share with us.

There's No Place Like Home!

Ultimately, the success or failure of our diversity recruitment (and retention) efforts will hinge on the individual employee's sense of personal welcome and inclusion within the day-to-day life of the organization. Regardless of skin color, gender, sexual preferences, age, or any other characteristic, individuals are attracted to or become committed to organizations in which they feel:

- Welcome and wanted
- Accepted and respected for who they are (and who they are becoming)
- Needed and effective ("my contribution counts")
- A sense of belonging—rather than me (or us) versus them
- Challenged
- Able to succeed (right tools, realistic objectives)
- A sense of heart-felt agreement with vision or mission
- Appreciated, recognized, and rewarded
- Whole and balanced
- Healthy and safe
- Treated fairly (compensation, opportunity for advancement)
- Listened to
- Pride (work, organization, peers, environment)

When all is said and done, I believe it is our common sense that will lead us toward a successful diversity recruitment and retention program.

▲ Note

1. Anonymous CEO quoted in "Moving Women of Color Up the Corporate Ladder," *Profiles in Diversity Journal,* May/June 2004.

CHAPTER 4

Hiring Success

As you know, a recruiter's job doesn't end with sourcing. We must also concern ourselves with the overall hiring process. In this chapter, we will examine:

- Partnering

- Planning the process

- Recruiting

- Candidate screening

- The application

- The interview

- Collateral material

- Background and reference checking

- The offer

- Paperwork

- Evaluation

How will we foster excellence throughout the hiring process? Let's take a look.

▲ **Strategy 42:** Partnering

Every hiring process begins with a hiring manager's initiation of a new requisition. The hiring manager holds the key to a successful recruiting effort. She dictates the requirements. She also decides to extend an offer of employment or send the recruiter back to the drawing board. Ideally, therefore, the hiring process will begin, proceed, and conclude with the recruiter and hiring manager working as partners.

Effective partnering begins with communication and mutual respect.

• *Take a genuine interest in your partners.* Don't wait for an open requisition to initiate dialogue with the hiring managers you serve. Schedule one-on-one time to explore ways that each of you can begin to appreciate the other's world. Explore ways that you may best work together toward anticipating future needs and recruitment strategies.

• *Be a pro.* Win the respect of others. Build a reputation for hard work, open and honest communication, great follow-up, and results. Hiring managers will gladly partner with such a professional.

• *Be assertive.* Maintain communication. Hold one another responsible for bringing creativity, candor, and communication to the partnership.

• *Show appreciation.* Remember to express appreciation for your partner's efforts. Partnering is critical to your success. Never take it for granted.

Finally, I want to point out that the concept of partnering applies to your peers, your support staff, your manager, and others who facilitate your success. Look beyond the buzzword *partnering* and reflect on creative ways to initiate, nurture, and maintain optimal personal and professional relationships. Partnering is no more—and no less—than the confluence of relationships and resources in pursuit of a common goal.

Strategy 43: Planning the Process

Considerable thought should be given to the creation of formal hiring processes, so have a plan and don't try to wing it. The questions posed during the operational audit (see Chapter 1) are an excellent place to start.

How Is a New Requisition Opened?

Generally, a standard requisition form should be utilized. It may be hard copy, or online via the HRIS system. It should include the following:

- Name of position
- Pay grade and level
- Department name
- Manager that position reports to
- Reason for opening
- Job description
- Required education, skills, and experience
- Desired education, skills, and experience
- Hiring manager's signature
- Authorization signature
- Date opened
- Needed by (target date)
- Recruiter's signature

Note: Ideally, the process should encourage hiring managers *and* recruiters to work together in the creation of each new requisition. Were more companies to involve HR and recruiting during the planning phase of each requisition, the entire recruiting and hiring process would run more smoothly.

How Are Requisitions Assigned to a Specific Recruiter?

Once the hiring manager has completed the requisition and forwarded it to the recruiting department, he or she may assume that work will begin immediately. In reality, this may or may not be the case. The process of assigning specific requisitions to specific recruiters should be clearly defined. I recommend doing the following:

• *Define an unambiguous requisition routing path.* Make sure that hiring managers know *exactly* how (and to whom) requisitions should be routed for delivery to the designated recruiter as quickly as possible.

• *Log each requisition.* Time-stamp each requisition upon its arrival within the recruiting department. This will create a definitive record of when the ball is in your court. The days-to-fill clock starts ticking at this point. In other words, don't charge yourself with the days-to-fill time before having the requisition physically in your possession.

Although an administrator may time-stamp requisitions upon their arrival at the departmental level, recruiters should not be charged with days-to-fill time prior to receiving the assignment from their manager. With this in mind, recruiters should time-stamp (date and initials) requisitions as they arrive on their desks. *Note:* Multiple time-stamps help in the identification of workflow breakdowns or bottlenecks should they arise.

- *Assign each requisition to a specific recruiter.* You may wish to assign requisitions based on *recruiter specialty*. IT requisitions are routed to IT recruiters. Nonexempt positions are routed to nonexempt recruiters. Executive-level searches are handled by executive recruiters, and so forth. Minimal bench strength makes specialty assignments unrealistic. Many organizations have only one or two recruiters to share the entire recruiting workload. In such instances, a *workload balance* strategy makes the most sense. Personally, I believe workload balancing always makes good sense—regardless of the number of recruiters on your team. I encourage specialty cross-training so that each recruiter can back up his or her fellow recruiters when necessary.

How Are Open Requisitions and Recruiting Activities Prioritized?

As a general rule, requisitions are acted on in the order they are received. There will be times, however, when common sense or an urgent situation demands a different prioritization strategy. Whenever recruiters have too many requisitions on their plates to give each one an appropriate amount of time and attention, I recommend the following:

- Reallocate requisitions to more evenly distribute the recruiter workload.
- Bring in temporary help (recruiters or administrative staff).
- Utilize research or third-part recruiting firms.
- Communicate openly and honestly with all hiring mangers and reach consensus regarding which requisitions are urgent and which can be put on the back burner.

Note: Be sure to have your clients (that is, the hiring managers) in the boat with you when making prioritization decisions. When you have a hiring manager's permission to put a requisition on hold, remember to freeze the days-to-fill clock until recruiting activity is resumed.

What Administrative Procedures Are Involved?

The hiring process will include a variety of administrative functions. The requisition form must be filled out and logged; advertisements must be written and placed; résumés must be collected, examined, and routed or filed. Interviews must be scheduled; rejection or offer letters sent; I-9, W-2, payroll, benefit, and other forms need to be filled out.

Each administrative task should be specifically assigned to an administrator, a recruiter, or a manager to ensure that every strategy is accounted for. It is also wise to ask, "Who is this specific task best assigned to?" Try to assign administrative tasks to administrators rather than to recruiters and recruiting managers. As mentioned earlier, more keypunching (and other administrative tasks) equals less recruiting.

How Are Candidates Sourced?

Chapter 2 is dedicated to exploring a variety of sourcing techniques. In the context of this discussion (regarding the hiring process), we should note that specific sourcing strategies are applied as needed to identify appropriate candidates. This means that we do not fly by the seat of our pants with each new requisition. The recruiting department that is dedicated to excellence will examine standard and creative sourcing techniques with a critical eye. What is working best for us? What is the most cost-effective? How might we improve?

How Are Candidates Screened?

Again, we should develop a specific blueprint and follow it toward ensuring consistent quality of work. We need to partner with hiring managers to identify specific screening criteria such as:

• *Required Skills and Credentials.* As previously discussed, the well-written requisition will differentiate between *required* and *desired* criteria. Our initial screening activities should focus on identification of requisite skills, education and experience.

• *Tests and Measurements.* Recruiters often utilize testing and measurement techniques to ascertain the level of candidate expertise. This may be a relatively informal process. For example, the hiring manager may prepare screening questions along with the specific answers we should hear from any qualified candidate. As recruiters, we simply administer the questionnaire and pass or fail candidates according to their answers.

We may wish to take a more formalized approach such as competency examinations for skills such as typing (speed and accuracy), math proficiency, and software-related skills, among others. *Note:* It is wise to run these tests and measurement instruments past legal counsel to minimize the risk of adverse impact liabilities.

When or How Are Candidates Introduced to the Hiring Manager?

I encourage recruiters to take ownership of every candidate introduced to a hiring manager. In other words, I recommend holding off on candidate introduction until the recruiter is personally excited about the candidate. I ask recruiters the following questions:

- Has the candidate met all prescreening criteria?
- Have you met with the candidate personally—by telephone *and* in-person when possible?
- Are you personally convinced that this candidate would be a great addition to your organization?
- If you are not convinced that is a great candidate, why would you ask the hiring manager to meet him or her?

Note: Obviously, there will be times when a recruiter is lukewarm about a candidate yet chooses to introduce this person anyway (if only for a second opinion). I don't have a problem with this. The term *taking ownership* means that recruiters won't introduce candidates without thoughtful consideration.

How or When Do Hiring Authorities Provide Feedback to Recruiters?

A lack of client feedback is the bane of the recruiting profession. It makes no difference whether you're an in-house corporate recruiter or an external headhunter—the lack of client feedback will drive you crazy on occasion. You invest considerable time and effort in finding the best candidates. You proudly and eagerly submit résumés to the hiring manager. Then, you wait and you wait and you wait for the hiring manager to get back to you. You are frustrated further each time a candidate calls to inquire: "So, have you heard anything yet?" You swallow the anger you feel welling up inside you with every unreturned voice mail and e-mail message. Crawling onto my soapbox for a moment, let me clearly state that I believe that there is no excuse for a lack of feedback.

- It is rude.
- It shows a lack of common courtesy and professionalism.
- It shows a lack of respect for both recruiter and candidate.

Enough said. I strongly urge you to work with your hiring managers and recruiters to reach a clear and up-front agreement concerning your mutual expectations regarding communication and feedback. Hold yourself and others accountable to deliver as promised.

How Are Hiring Decisions Made?

The decision to extend an offer is the moment of truth in the hiring process.

Before reaching this moment, we should have methodically touched all the following bases:

- Prescreen and interview due diligence
- Key constituency buy-in
- Background and reference checks
- "Test close" positioning to avoid surprises
- Appropriate authorization

How Is an Offer or Notice of Rejection Conveyed to Candidates?

- *Form.* Thoughtful consideration should be given to offer and rejection letter language. We will be taking a close look at the topic of offer letters in Strategy 49. Here, let's examine the rejection letter as an equally important element in recruiting excellence. You will send out significantly more rejection letters than offer letters. Take time to create rejection letters that:

1. ***Convey a Genuine Sense of Gratitude.*** "Thank you very much for considering our company. We sincerely appreciate your interest."

2. ***Let the Candidate Down Gently.*** "We have enjoyed a most gratifying response to the advertisement for our open programmer/analyst position. Although your résumé was not among the few that we believe most closely met the requirements for this particular position, we were nonetheless very impressed with your background."

3. ***Encourage the Candidate.*** "We wish you success in your career search and trust you will find a great opportunity in the near future. Thanks again for you interest!"

• ***Conveyance.*** Assign specific personnel to ensure timely and consistent follow-up. Excellence is the result of disciplined effort en route to predictable outcomes!

▲ **Strategy 44:** Recruiting

After having sourced appropriate candidates, how do we go about recruiting them? The recruiting process involves the following steps:

Appropriate Planning and Processes (See Chapter 1)

Many recruiting operations rely on sketchy requisition details to create equally sketchy sourcing strategies. They run an advertisement in the Sunday newspaper. They post the opening on the Internet. They sit back and wait for résumés to arrive. They forward those that appear to be in the ballpark onto the hiring manager and call it a day. This begs the question "How can we recruit effectively if we don't know what we're looking for?"

Recruiters who are committed to excellence must sweat the details. Once again, *crawl into your client's world* to develop a thorough appreciation of the habitat, watering holes, and idiosyncrasies of the particular lion you are being asked to hunt.

Sourcing

Armed with adequate requisition detail, we may creatively apply a combination of traditional and creative sourcing techniques to identify appropriate candidates (see Chapter 2).

Initial Contact

During our initial contact with a candidate, we tend to focus on the *first impression* he or she is making on us. This is a natural and valuable response. We need to remember that the candidate's first impression of us (and of our company) is equally important.

From the moment we introduce ourselves, we are selling our company. Don't ruin your chances for a great hire over a lack of attention to the first impression *you* are making!

Candidate Screening

As you undoubtedly know, there are a variety of federal, state, and local laws that prohibit discrimination in hiring practices. Perhaps best known is Title VII of the Civil Rights Act. Title VII outlaws any employment action (including hiring, terminations, and promotions, among others) that discriminate against the protected classes of race, color, national origin, religion, and gender. The Age Discrimination in Employment Act of 1967, (ADEA), added all persons over the age of forty to the ranks of protected class candidates and employees.

Prescreening tests and measurements are used to narrow the field of candidates to those whose skills and knowledge appear to best match requisition requirements. Unfortunately, there are times when a specific test or measurement instrument may be shown to have had an adverse impact on a protected class of candidate.

How is adverse impact determined? *Adverse impact* may have occurred when the selection rate of a *protected* class is less than 80 percent of the class with the highest selection rate. ***Note:*** *Selection* refers to any and all terms and conditions of employment from hiring to promotions, educational opportunities, terminations, and more. For example, let's assume that 120 candidates have applied for the same position and 100 candidates are Caucasian and 20 are minority candidates. We give the exact same candidate-screening test to all 120 candidates with the following results:

- 52 percent of the Caucasian candidates (52 out of 100) receive a passing score.

- 35 percent of the minority candidates (7 out of 20) receive a passing score.

Here is the tricky part, because we need to ask ourselves, "What is 80 percent of the highest selection rate?" In this example, the Caucasians are the group with the highest selection rate. We must ask, "What is 80 percent of the 52 percent Caucasian selection rate?" The answer is that 80 percent of 52 percent = 41.6 percent. Since the percentage of minority candidates with passing scores (35 percent) is less than 80 percent of the highest rate of selection (41.6 percent), *adverse impact* is said to exist and your company may be vulnerable to a discrimination lawsuit.

As with all employment practices, please remember to coordinate candidate-screening efforts with legal counsel to avoid potential liability.

Selling the Opportunity

Again, selling the opportunity begins with the initial contact. We need to be friendly, courteous, knowledgeable, and enthusiastic.

- *Friendly and Courteous.* An initial contact or interview situation can be intimidating. The candidate is wondering, "Is this the type of company I want to work for? Will I get along with these people? Do I like them? Will they like me?" The recruiter's friendly and courteous demeanor goes a long way toward easing initial fears. A relaxed candidate is better able to put his or her best foot forward and engage in an objective assessment of the opportunity.

- **Knowledgeable.** The more the recruiter knows about each particular opportunity, and the company in general, the better. The knowledgeable recruiter is prepared to facilitate candidate assessment of the opportunity. He or she is also prepared to differentiate between qualified and unqualified prospects.

- **Enthusiastic.** Attitude is contagious. The recruiter's personal enthusiasm for the company and the opportunity (or lack thereof) is readily apparent. When the recruiter is genuinely excited about the opportunity, the candidate will be inclined to view it more positively as well.

Pre-Closing Candidates for Hiring Authority

Let's imagine that, having remembered to work with legal counsel so as to avoid potential adverse impact liability, we administered screening tests to several candidates. We then determined that a select number of these candidates have passed and are qualified for introduction to the hiring manager. Rather than simply passing the résumé along to the hiring manager, the heads-up recruiter will use this moment as an opportunity to pre-close (sell) the candidate:

- **Give feedback.** "There appears to be an excellent match between your qualifications and our requirements."

- **Be enthusiastic.** This is an excellent opportunity to encourage candidate enthusiasm by way of your own: "I'm really excited about introducing you to Mary Jones. This position reports to Mary and I think the two of you will really hit it off. You have a lot in common. Folks love working with Mary and I believe you would fit in perfectly with the rest of the team."

- *Provide collateral material.* Anticipate candidate questions and concerns. Walk them through general (rather than specific) discussion regarding compensation and benefits, company culture, and operations. Make sure they have access to the annual report, company website, and any additional material that will help them prepare for their interviews.

- *Test the waters.* Ask, "What about this opportunity appeals to you?" and "What questions/concerns do you have at this time?" Don't neglect these pre-close questions *prior to introducing the candidate* to the hiring manager. If a candidate is not serious, it's best to find out now.

Staying with the Process Until Closed

The recruiting process is not complete until the requisition has been successfully filled. Even then, recruiters are well advised to stay in touch with newly hired employees to help ensure a smooth on-boarding process.

Having introduced the candidate to the hiring manager, the recruiter should remain in close contact to facilitate interview and hiring decision processes:

- *Coordinate offer and acceptance details.* The recruiter should remain active as a liaison between hiring authority and candidate during the negotiation process as needed.

- *Communicate rejection notice.* Messages of "thanks but no thanks" should be done with sensitivity and tact. Be prompt, courteous, and professional. Don't keep candidates hanging. Even a rejected candidate deserves personal and professional respect. It's a small world. Discourteous treatment of candidates may damage the reputation of both recruiter and company—rightly so.

• *Refine requisition requirements and search strategy.* Take advantage of hiring authority feedback concerning every rejected candidate to refine your search.

Keep your head in the game.

▲ **Strategy 45:** The Employment Application Form

Critical examination of the employment application form is an often overlooked strategy on the road to recruiting excellence. Take a look at yours. Is it well designed? Does form efficiently compliment function?

The typical employment application form is poorly designed, as shown in Figure 4-1.

Do yourself, your candidates, and your company a favor by examining your company's employment application form. Fill one out yourself and ask other willing recruiters and staff to do the same. Keep a separate sheet of notepaper nearby for improvement ideas. As you work your way through the application, ask yourself the following questions:

- Is it functional and easy to use?

- Is every question really necessary (would a résumé suffice)?

- Does the application provide reasonable space for requested information?

- Have we run the form past legal counsel for their input?

- Is the form professional looking (pleasing to the eye)?

- Would we be proud to show this form to our customers, shareholders, and industry peers?

FIGURE 4-1. REMEMBER TO PROVIDE ADEQUATE SPACE.

In the space below give a detailed description of current job responsibilities (please write legibly):

IS ENOUGH SPACE PROVIDED?

- Is there a better way to handle this (perhaps with an online application)?

Use common sense and creativity to make sure that your employment application has the appearance, functionality, and ease of use that you desire. Work with counsel to ensure that it covers the necessary disclaimer and compliance language.

All application forms are not created equal. This is painfully evident when today's job seeker fills out the typical online application. Again, the so-called norm is a cumbersome and confusing series of screens with harsh commands such as "WARNING: You *must* complete the following fields!"

The minutiae requested by the required fields are often absurd if not downright illegal. For example, I've seen a number of sites with mandatory fields such as the month and the year of high school graduation (an open invitation for the applicant to initiate an age-discrimination lawsuit).

Whenever I see an especially poor design, I generally suspect that some HR manager got together with an IT developer and provided him or her with a long list of "must have" and "nice to have" requirements. The well-meaning IT staff develops an online form that includes every item requested without much thought (or concern) regarding how the employment application will actually be used by the hapless candidates who have to complete it.

As with your hard-copy application, take time to fill out a copy of your company's online employment application. Enlist other staff to do the same. Compare notes and brainstorm regarding how to improve it.

Is It Intuitive?

Can you find the employment application easily? Many companies bury their job-search database and application forms deep within a maze of company Web pages.

Although it is fictional, the following story is *not* atypical:

Jim is a recruiter who is visiting the website of XYZ Corporation in hopes of finding an open position that he might personally apply for. He notices a small CAREERS button in the upper right hand corner of XYZ's homepage. Jim clicks on the link and intuitively believes that he is headed in the right direction. Wrong! Rather than an application or list of open jobs, Jim finds a sales pitch entitled "Why consider a Career with XYZ Company?" At the end of the pitch, there is another button: JOBS AT XYZ. He presses this button suspecting that *now* he will find what he's looking for. Wrong again! This button takes him to a page that asks: "What kind of job are you looking for?" along with separate buttons for human resources, information technology, administration, and executive, among others. Because recruiting falls within HR, Jim clicks on HUMAN RESOURCES as he thinks to himself, "Now, I'm getting somewhere." Oops! Not so fast. This button yields a pitch on the virtues of a career in XYZ's HR department. On and on and on it goes. Eventually, Jim manages to somehow stumble upon an area that actually allows him to search current openings. He finds a number of drop-down menus to facilitate his search. "What type of job are you looking for?" Jim clicks on the menu and scrolls down to HUMAN RESOURCES. "Where would you like to work?" Jim is open to relocation so anywhere will do. Rather than choosing a geographical preference from the provided drop-down menu, he clicks SEARCH. A message pops up: "WARNING: you must select a geographical area." Seeing that there is no ANY/ALL option available to him, Jim must now select one state at a time (in other words fifty separate searches!) to see all available HR openings. What a nightmare.

Is Your Online Application User-Friendly?

Candidates should be able to easily move from one section of the application to another. For example, a candidate should be able to jump forward or backward without pop-up warnings or loss of previously keypunched information. If you feel you really need warnings at all, save them for the final send stage of the process.

Does your application allow a variety of data input options, such as cut-and-paste, keypunch, and drop-down menus? Can a candidate cut and paste résumé sections or must he or she retype this same information?

Do application drop-down menus help or hinder the application flow? Many online applications have a variety of drop-down menus (some are more helpful than others). The logic of the U.S. state drop-down menu eludes me. Common sense suggests that it is easier to type a two-letter state abbreviation than it is to click and scroll. When the letter *M,* is typed, the menu will often jump to Maine. Hit *M* a second time and the menu jumps to Maryland. A third *M* will bring up Massachusetts. God help the hapless candidate from Montana. She would need to execute nine inputs (one click plus eight *M*s) to get to the right state. **Note:** You may wish to add a drop-down menu of abbreviations as an adjacent help link for the rare candidate who doesn't know his or her state abbreviation. You need to ask the following questions:

- Are the instructions clear?
- Is each section necessary?

Many online applications request academic grade-point averages (from high school, college, and graduate studies). I often wonder how often a grade-point average influences a company's interest (or lack thereof) in a particular candidate. I also wonder whether companies differentiate between a *C* at Harvard and an *A* at ABC Community College. Do they differentiate between the *A* student whose parents footed the tuition bill and the *B* student who held down a full-time job while working his way through college? Does anyone even bother to ask such questions? If not, why not?

My point here is simply to encourage you to really think about what types of information you need to collect. Take time to formulate a specific and legitimate rationale for the data you request. Excellence is found in common sense.

▲ Strategy 46: The Interview

Hundreds of books have been written on the topic of how to conduct an effective interview. I won't attempt to cover similar ground here. I do want to point out, however, I believe well-designed and implemented interview processes are critical to the success of your recruiting program.

The interview is often *the* deciding-factor regarding whether or not a candidate will be offered a position. After all the sourcing, screening, background checks, and references are complete, it is often the interviewer's gut feeling that swings the decision one way or another: "I like her. I think she would be a great addition to the team;" or "I don't know. I don't see a good fit here. I think we should pass."

In other words, when all is said and done, hiring tends to be a rather subjective decision. Certainly, subjective considerations *should* be taken into account. After all, the hiring manager knows the company and knows what he's looking for. A new hire needs to get along with others and fit in with rest of the group if she is to have a happy and successful career with the company. On the other hand, subjective decisions may not always be fair to the candidate. They also may not be the correct or best decision. As long as human beings are involved in the hiring process, subjectivity will play a significant role. Still, we can build objectivity safeguards into the hiring process.

I am a proponent of behavioral interviewing. This is an interviewing methodology that focuses on exploration of a candidate's past behavior as a predictive indicator of future behavior. Specific requirements of an open requisition are framed as behavioral questions. For example, if the individual we hope to hire must be able to meet deadlines while working under a great deal of pressure, we might inquire: "Tell me about a time when you met a deadline while working under extreme pressure."

If you need someone who is proficient with Excel spreadsheets, you might ask: "Tell me about a time when you designed or revised an Excel spreadsheet to track mission-critical data."

Behavioral interview questions are open-ended. Candidates are encouraged to give specific examples and detail. By comparison, close-ended questions encourage either a yes or no response. For example, "Have you ever worked under pressure to meet a deadline?" or "Have you worked with Excel?" A trip to your local bookstore, library, or Internet search engine will provide you with readily available resources regarding behavioral interviewing and other interview methodologies.

Recruiting professionals must also be mindful of our responsibility to ensure that our interview and selection methods are in compliance with state and federal employment law. As we take a look at this sensitive area of recruitment, remember I am not an attorney. Please consult a lawyer if you want professional assurance that my information, and your interpretation of it, is appropriate to your particular situation.

State law tends to reinforce federal law. Employers are prohibited from using employment advertising that limits or indicates applicant preference based on age, race, color, religion, sex, or national origin (or sexual orientation in some states). Take time to familiarize yourself with several key federal laws that work in concert to prohibit employment discrimination (directly affecting recruitment and hiring practices).

- Title VII of the Civil Rights Act of 1964 (Title VII) prohibits employment discrimination based on race, color, religion, sex, or national origin.

- The Equal Pay Act of 1963 (EPA) protects men and women who perform substantially equal work in the same establishment from sex-based wage discrimination.

- The Age Discrimination in Employment Act of 1967 (ADEA) protects individuals who are forty years of age or older.

- Title I and V of Americans with Disabilities Act of 1990 (ADA) prohibits employment discrimination against qualified individuals with disabilities in the private sector, and in state and local governments.

- Sections 501 and 505 of the Rehabilitation Act of 1973 prohibit discrimination against qualified individuals with disabilities who work in the federal government.

- The Civil Rights Act of 1991 provides—among other things—monetary damages in cases of intentional employment discrimination.

These laws have a direct impact on the interview process regarding the types of questions that may or may not be asked of candidates. The Equal Employment Opportunity Commission (EEOC) provides a wealth of information to help us navigate the murky waters.

For example, the Americans with Disabilities Act (ADA) and the Rehabilitation Act of 1973 (amended) prohibit discrimination in employment on basis of handicap. The EEOC informs us that while it is lawful to ask an applicant to explain how he or she would perform the tasks with or without reasonable accommodations, it is unlawful to ask "Do you have any disabilities, defects, or on-the-job injuries?" In that minorities tend to experience poverty more than the average white person, consideration of credit factors tends to have an adverse effect on minorities. Thus, all questions regarding credit rating, charge accounts, garnishments, or other indebtedness are unlawful. Although inquires pertaining to these same areas may lawfully be made within the context of a postoffer background check, any adverse action arising from such investigation triggers the applicant's Fair Credit Reporting Act rights. Visit the State of Idaho's website http://cl.idaho.gov/lawintvw3.htm or the State of Colorado's http://www.cde.state.co.us/cdechart/download/ HREmploymentManual.pdf (see pages 40 to 46) for excellent overviews of how to conduct lawful employment interviews.

Review current interviewing processes by asking the following questions:

- Do we have a specific interview methodology or are we winging it?
- Is implementation organized, coordinated, effective, and legally compliant?
- Are interviews fairly weighted in comparison with our other candidate-screening and selection techniques?
- Have we sought the opinion of legal counsel to ensure that our interview methodology won't expose us to unnecessary liability risks (that is, do we know to avoid illegal questions regarding age, race, religion, and so forth)?
- Is there a better way to handle interviews?

Examine the answers with a critical eye. Design and implement change where needed.

▲ **Strategy 47:** Collateral Material

I find it strange that the very company that pinches pennies spent on recruiting-related collateral material will often readily pay exorbitant third-party fees when its internal recruitment efforts fail. I repeat, "Excellence is in the details." Examine your supply of collateral material (brochures, annual reports, benefit summaries, and the like). Carefully go over each individual piece and ask yourself:

- Is this piece well written?
- What questions does it answer?
- What questions does it raise?
- Is this piece well designed (attractive and easy to read and understand)?
- Does it convey useful information or fluff?
- What does it tell a potential candidate about the type of company we are?
- How does it help a candidate make an informed decision about joining us?

We rarely ask these questions. Too often, we hand out a piece of collateral material simply because it's there. Excellence is found in intentionality.

▲ **Strategy 48:** Background and Reference Checking

Thorough background and reference checks are essential to intelligent hiring decisions. They are also an especially sensitive, and at times complicated, aspect of the hiring process. In order to touch all appropriate bases while safeguarding candidate and company rights and interests, I often recommend outsourcing some or all of the background- and reference-checking procedures to experts in these particular fields.

- The following Yahoo search yields about 1,610,000 hits: **"Background Check" employment**

- Adding state name will narrow the results: **"Background Check" employment Ohio**

- Add city to narrow results further: **"Background Check" employment Ohio Cleveland**

As always, use quotation marks and keyword combinations to drill down to the specific information you are seeking. In this case, the 1,610,000 hits have been narrowed to 31,700 hits by adding the words *Ohio* and *Cleveland*. **Note:** Federal law protects individuals (including candidates) from invasion of privacy. Before your company collects a credit report, drug test, polygraph, medical information, or other background and reference information, coordinate these efforts with legal counsel to ensure that you are adhering to guidelines as specified in federal, state, and local legislation, such as:

- The Consumer Credit Protection Act (1968)
- The Privacy Act (1974)

- The Fair Credit Reporting Act (1970)

- The Employee Polygraph Protection Act (1988)

Make sure that legal counsel has reviewed and approved all screening activities to include background and reference checks.

▲ Strategy 49: The Offer

An effective offer letter will balance the following elements:

- *Genuine Welcoming Language.*

"We are pleased to offer you the position of . . ."

"We look forward to working with you."

"Welcome aboard!"

- *Compensation and Position Specificity.* "We are pleased to offer you the position of senior credit analyst in our Commercial Equipment Leasing division reporting to Mary Smith. We look forward to your first day of work with us on January 2, 2007. You will receive a base salary of $2,307.70 paid biweekly, which computes to an annual salary of $60,000. We are also pleased to offer you a variety of fringe benefits that you will become eligible for according to the provisions, limitations, and enrollment procedures of each plan."

- *Disclaimers and Liability Protection.* Work with legal counsel to insert appropriate "at will employment" and "contingent offer of employment" language regarding references, drug screen, noncompete agreement, and so forth.

Note: Be sure to build quality-assurance protection into your offer letter conveyance processes. Have the recruiter *and* hiring manager review each offer letter before sending it out. I know of several examples where the importance of this lesson was learned the hard way via *very* expensive misunderstandings between recruiter and hiring manager concerning offer terms and conditions.

▲ **Strategy 50:** Paperwork

The hiring process creates a variety of paperwork that must be tracked and filed. As with other areas of HR, the federal government has passed legislation that affects hiring-related record keeping. From EEO reports and Affirmative Action plans to application, payroll, benefits and general employment-record retention, the road to recruiting excellence must include planning and execution of effective paperwork-management processes, procedures, and systems.

We need to be familiar with specific record-management requirements that are applicable to our particular organization. For example, The Age Discrimination in Employment Act (ADEA) requires that employers with twenty or more employees retain payroll and other employment records for three years.

The Americans with Disabilities Act (ADA) requires employers with fifteen or more employees to retain personnel records pertaining to all requests for "reasonable accommodation" as well as records related to promotions, demotions, layoff, termination, and other employment actions. These records must be retained for at least one year from the date of the specific employment action taken.

The Equal Pay Act requires three-year retention of all payroll records (timesheets, payroll deductions, wage rate information, and more).

The Fair Labor Standards Act (FLSA) requires three-year retention of records that specify each employee's name, address, date of birth, gender, and occupation as well as a variety of pay and hour-related data.

The Immigration Reform and Control Act requires that Employee Eligibility Verification Forms (I-9) be kept for the longer of "three years from date of hire" or one year from termination of employment.

Believe it or not, these are but a few of the many laws to which we must adhere.

As always, work closely with legal counsel to ensure that appropriate compliance strategies and safeguards are in place.

▲ **Strategy 51:** Evaluation

No hiring process is complete without the capstone of evaluation. The evaluation process may be formal or informal. It must nonetheless entail an open, honest, and constructively critical look at the recently completed hiring activity. An evaluation seeks to answer the questions: How did we do? What have we learned? How might we improve?

• *Partnering.* Did we maintain an optimal level of communication and cooperation with all parties involved?

• *Planning the Process.* Did we have a plan? Was our plan helpful? Was it realistic? Was it comprehensive and adequate to the tasks before us?

• *Recruiting.* Did we take time to adequately understand the requisition? Did we partner effectively with the hiring manager to gain appropriate insight? Did our policies and procedures facilitate timely and effective work flow? What sourcing techniques were effective? What sourcing techniques did not prove to be especially effective? Did we do an appropriate job of selling the opportunity to each candidate? Did we stay on top of things and follow up?

• *Candidate Screening.* Were our screening techniques fair and effective? Did we coordinate screening efforts with legal counsel to minimize our liability risks?

• *The Application.* Are our application forms and processes user-friendly? Do they capture the information we want or need without requiring superfluous data? Do they contain appropriate release and disclaimer language?

- **The Interview.** Did we apply a specific methodology? Did we seek and coordinate feedback among different interviewer-team members? Were our interviews helpful and efficient? Did we work with counsel or have adequate prior training to avoid illegal questions?

- **Collateral Material.** What collateral material did we hand out? Was it helpful? Has a recent review of all such material convinced us that each specific piece has a legitimate and helpful function? Does each piece represent us in the manner that best reflects our organization brand?

- **Background and Reference Checking.** Did we check background and references prior to making an offer? Has legal counsel endorsed our background- and reference-checking strategies?

- **The Offer.** Did the offer process go smoothly? If not, why not? Did the offer letter balance welcome, detail, and legal considerations effectively?

- **Paperwork.** Have we captured and cataloged all necessary paperwork?

Pathways to excellence are often discovered through evaluation.

CHAPTER 5

Retention Success

In Chapter 1, we examine a general overview of recruiting. In Chapter 2, we examine a variety of sourcing strategies. Chapter 3 explores hiring processes from the recruiter's perspective. Chapter 4 encourages a common-sense approach to diversity. Still, our job is not done. We must also take employee retention concerns into consideration. Without a successful employee retention program, we bring new employees in the front door as experienced employees walk out the back door. Net progress can be compromised. Let's look at a number of steps we can take to reinforce our companies' employee retention efforts:

- Onboarding
- Mentoring
- Building a sense of community
- Recognition and rewards
- Involvement

- Training and development
- Keeping your promises
- The report card
- Performance appraisals
- Just ask!
- Exit interviews
- Golden handcuffs
- Anti-raiding strategies
- Culture
- Environment

▲ **Strategy 52:** Onboarding

A sound employee retention program begins the moment each new employee reports for his or her first day of work. I recommend formal "onboarding" processes that address the following considerations:

Making the New Employee Feel Welcome

Take steps to ensure that new employees are expected. Encourage staff to introduce themselves and make each new employee feel welcome.

Advance Preparations

Make sure the new employee's workspace is ready to receive him or her. Make sure a computer has been set up with the appropriate software, e-mail, and printing capabilities. Make sure that the new employee's telephone extension and voicemail have been activated. Have a copy of the latest employee directory on his or her desk. Make sure the desk has been stocked with an initial supply of pens, pencils, scissors, stapler, staples, and staple remover. Make sure paper, sticky notes, notepads, and folders are readily available. Have a temporary supply of business cards ready to go.

New employees will appreciate the attention to detail invested toward getting them off on the right foot.

New-Hire Checklist

Create a new-hire checklist and assign a specific administrator to make sure that everything is in place.

Item Check upon Completion

Employee Handbook _____

Policy Procedure Manual _____

Payroll and Benefits Enrollment _____

Confidentiality Agreement _____

Noncompete Agreement _____

Supplies (use separate checklist) _____

Phone and Voicemail Extension _____

Computer System and E-mail _____

Internet and Intranet Access _____

Orientation Meeting Schedules _____

Mentor Assigned _____

Team Introductions _____

Other: _____ (add items specific to your organization)

Pairing an experienced employee with a new employee is a smart way to facilitate newcomer success. The established employee is able to show the ropes to the new employee and bring him or her up to speed in of the following areas:

• *Job Expectations/Methods.* "Our official hours are 9 to 5; most of us get here by 8:00 and leave between 5:30 and 6:00 at night. Let me show you show our HRIS works. Let's go look over our policy and procedure manuals. I want to give you a few pointers."

• *Cultural Lay of the Land.* "Things have been a little tense around here since the announcement that some of the departments in this building will be relocating across town. Don't worry. It doesn't affect us. By the way, some of us go out for a beer after work every Wednesday. You're welcome to join us. Fridays are bagel days. We take turns bringing bagels and doughnuts. We also have a lotto pool you might want to get in on."

• *Physical Resource Familiarization.* "The coffee machine is here. The supply cabinet is there. Restrooms are located halfway down that corridor. The copier and fax machine are over here. If you need any administrative support, Sally here will help you. Your office is here and mine is down the hall to the right. Our weekly staff meetings are held Monday mornings at 7:30 in the first conference room on your left."

A buddy system is invaluable to orientation and integration success.

▲ **Strategy 54:** Building a Sense of Community

An effective mentoring relationship gets new employees headed in the right direction. A sense of community and a feeling of belonging are enhanced when we take time to:

- Celebrate birthdays

- Celebrate work anniversaries

- Create a variety of reward and recognition programs

- Create company sports teams

- Hold company and family picnics and outings

- Create high-visibility vision, mission, and goal statements

- Support local charities with company or departmental volunteer groups

- Participate in "Take Our Daughters And Sons To Work Day"

- Have Halloween and other holiday parties

Apply creativity to the discovery of new, meaningful, and fun ways to help each employee enjoy strong community identity. A sense of belonging within the larger community is critical to employee retention.

▲ **Strategy 55:** Recognition and Rewards

I don't know who coined the phrase "Catch your employees doing something right!" but I think it is brilliant advice. Employees don't leave their personal lives at home when they head off to work each morning. They bring their hopes, dreams, happiness, and pain to work with them. They have good days and bad. They long for encouragement. They are sensitive to criticism.

Employees need to feel safe and valued. This is especially true when times are tough (market turmoil, organizational upheaval). We tend to have little difficulty finding ways to ask our employees to improve performance. "Catching" them doing something right is a simple but effective way to convey that we also recognize their positive contributions. For example, you might say the following:

- "Nice job on your report this morning!"
- "Tom Wilson said you did a terrific job filling his latest requisition."
- "That's a great idea! You are very creative."
- "You did a beautiful job of handling a tough situation. Nice work!"

Recognition may take on a more formal look:

- Employee of the Month (certificate on wall, story in company newsletter, and so forth)
- Public praise (announcing individual accomplishments to team or company)
- Letters of recognition

Whether formal or informal, we appreciate it when our efforts are recognized. Recognition boosts morale and motivates excellence. It is a cornerstone of effective employee retention.

Be creative! Recognize progress and improvement. Recognize dedication, hard work, and examples of going the extra mile. Recognize years of service with employment anniversaries. Recognize acts of kindness and team spirit. In other words, be generous with recognition and praise. Take advantage of all opportunities to reinforce actions and behaviors that will further your team's progress toward excellence.

Think about ways to expand your employee recognition programs.

The concepts of *recognition* and *reward* are interlinked. Recognition may be thought of as a form of psychological reward. Rewards are the tangible form of recognition. Again, I encourage you to be generous with recognition and reward toward reinforcing desired behavior. A reward can be in the form of a pat on the back or a cash bonus. It may be a plaque or a promotion. Take a look at these common examples, and think of creative additions to the list:

- Cash bonus

- Raise

- Promotion

- Plaque

- Preferred parking space (typically for a week or a month)

- Time off

- Extra vacation days

- Gift certificate

- Trip for two

- Invitation to "circle of excellence" conference or event

An entire industry has evolved to assist employers with creative reward and recognition programs. Fire up your trusty Internet search engine to identify reward and recognition services in you area. For example, Maritz Rewards (http://www.maritz rewards.com) offers a selection of more than 1,600 merchandise items, ranging in value from $25 to $9,000. These companies are an excellent source of novel ideas that you may wish to incorporate into your reward and recognition program.

▲ **Strategy 56:** Involvement

Employee retention efforts are bolstered when employees are emotionally invested in their company. Emotional investment is often enhanced when employees are allowed meaningful involvement in the decisions affecting their daily lives and their future. Here are a few suggestions to increase employee involvement.

Employee Referral Program

As we've seen, an effective employee referral system benefits recruiting by way of additional sourcing muscle. It benefits employees by way of referral bonus monies and recognition. It also benefits employee retention efforts in that it gives the employee who has made a successful referral an emotional stake in the new employee and the general well-being of the company. The more individuals I have personally recruited into the company, the greater my sense of personal impact.

Committee and Task Force Participation

Employees who volunteer for (or are appointed to) a special committee or task force duty generally come out of the experience with an enhanced sense of emotional involvement (positive or negative). Committee work can be very rewarding. Participants believe they have made a difference. They take pride in knowing that positive changes will come about as a direct result of their efforts. On the other hand, it can be frustrating when management does not support or act on committee findings and recommendations. This is a case of "we asked you to help us solve this problem and now we are going to ignore your recommendations."

When management is dedicated to supporting committee efforts, employees feel empowered, appreciated, and heard. I highly recommend selective and creative use of committee and task force groups to enhance employee involvement, satisfaction, and retention.

Note: Unionized organizations need to work closely with legal counsel to ensure that any such employee groups do not constitute an unfair labor practice.

Community Meetings

Presidential politics have popularized the town meeting in recent years. I believe such open-forum meetings would also serve corporate America well. They would encourage communication, involvement, and identification with the greater community. They would allow management to proactively respond to employee questions and concerns. They would be a platform from which to test the waters regarding new ideas and directions.

Community and Team Efforts

As mentioned earlier, a variety of activities (sport teams, company picnics, charity fund-raising drives, and so forth) help build employees' sense of community. Still, there is a difference between a sense of community and a sense of belonging within that community. Management should promote and encourage active employee participation to foster individual sense of belonging. Employees are reluctant to leave a company where they sense that they belong.

▲ **Strategy 57:** Training and Development

We have previously looked at the importance of training and development for furthering the professional competence of our recruiters. I mention training and development in this context in that I believe they are especially important to successful employee retention efforts. Training and development initiatives are an investment in the employee. As such, they signal the following:

- We believe in you.
- We believe that you are an intelligent and capable professional.
- We are committed to your success—today and in the future.
- We are investing in your acquisition of new skills. We are investing in the enhancement of today's skill set in preparation for tomorrow's challenges and responsibilities.
- We are evolving.

No one wants to stay with a stagnant organization. Our world changes rapidly and organizations must change with it or perish. Training and development programs send a message: "Our company is looking ahead and we are committed to our continued relevance and viability in the competitive marketplace."

Training and development are investments in employee retention.

▲ **Strategy 58:** Keep Your Promises

Employee retention increases with employee confidence in management. Relationships are built on mutual trust and respect. Everyone is on his or her best behavior during the interview and hiring process. In this regard, it is similar to the courtship period before marriage. Once the honeymoon is over, it is easy to forget yesterday's good intentions.

I recommend taking meticulous notes regarding the promises made during the recruiting and hiring process. For example, you might say:

- "We'll review you at six months."
- "You'll be eligible for a bonus at the end of the year."
- "You'll be eligible for promotion after the first six months."
- "We'll make sure that you receive additional training."

Employee retention suffers whenever employees become disillusioned with management and no longer trust that expectations will be met. Don't be sloppy with details. Don't put your employees in the awkward position of having to remind management of promises made.

Over the years, I have routinely asked candidates the question: "Why would you consider a career move at this time?" All too frequently, the answer given for wanting to leave a current employer is related to broken promises. "My company has not followed through with the raise, promotion, training and development (whatever) they promised me."

Don't let employee morale and retention suffer over promises made and broken. Don't commit to things that you do not intend to *meticulously* follow through with.

▲ **Strategy 59:** The Report Card

As pointed out previously regarding the customer satisfaction survey, it is smart to regularly gauge our performance through the eyes of the folks we serve. Formal online or hard-copy surveys should allow respondents to be anonymous to increase the likelihood of a candid response. Informal feedback should be encouraged through open-forum dialogue at departmental and company town meetings. The suggestion box, letters to the editor (company newsletter), employee satisfaction surveys, and 360-degree performance appraisals are among the more common methods used measure employee satisfaction.

I recommend a combination of formal and informal methodologies. I also believe these report cards should be evaluated at regular intervals throughout the year. Keep in mind that open-ended questions such as the following will generally provide more valuable information than yes or no and "on a scale of 1 to 10" type surveys.

- What are we doing well?
- Where do we need to improve?
- What specific actions might we take to initiate such improvement?
- What obstacles might we encounter?
- How might we best overcome these obstacles?
- Any other suggestions?

Employee retention is ultimately a report card in and of itself. High employee turnover is an indication that something is wrong.

Low turnover is an indicator that employees are generally satisfied.

Fortunately, we need not leave employee satisfaction to chance or speculation. Through regular and creative application of employee satisfaction surveys we can monitor the pulse of the community. When we frequently request employee feedback, analyze the results, and implement appropriate changes toward improving employee satisfaction, employee retention will take care of itself.

▲ **Strategy 60:** Performance Appraisals

Entire books have been written on the topic of performance appraisal. My contribution to the topic shall be limited to discussing performance appraisal in the context of employee retention. For better or worse, your company's performance appraisal methodologies will influence its employee retention efforts. To ensure that performance appraisals help rather than hurt employee retention efforts, I recommend the following:

No Surprises!

Tie performance appraisals to goals and objectives that have been clearly articulated at the *beginning* of the performance appraisal period. It is unfair to spring previously unstated objectives on employees while handing them their appraisals. As obvious as this may sound, companies often hold employees accountable for retroactive objectives. Such surprises are a surefire way to hurt employee retention.

Objective Assessment

Tie evaluation to measurable performance. For example, you might say: "At the beginning of this quarter we agreed that you would work toward improving your days-to-fill ratio from forty-five to thirty days or less. I have given you a 'needs improvement' rating in this area in that your days-to-fill ratio has not changed."

In the previous example, the rating is unfavorable but fair. When employee retention is negatively affected in such an instance it is generally because an employee does not feel especially secure in his job when his performance rating is below average.

He may look to leave prior to an anticipated termination. ***Note:*** Companies typically welcome turnover of employees who cannot achieve or maintain adequate levels of performance.

Thoughtful Methodology

Performance appraisals are often poorly designed and executed. It is generally easy to differentiate *excellent* from *poor* performance. It is not as easy to measure and evaluate the shades of gray. I encourage you to visit a variety of Internet sites that address this topic. Type "performance appraisals" into your favorite search engine for reference material (remember to bracket the term in quotation marks). Use terms such as "360," "effective," or "best practice" to narrow results.

Use It or Lose It

Use a performance appraisal as a development tool. A performance appraisal should be an open, honest, and constructive exchange between the participants. It is an opportunity to review past performance while specifying expectations of improved performance where necessary. Eliminate performance appraisals that are an exercise in going through the motions. Take time to question the way we've always done things and build a performance appraisal methodology that is fair and effective. Employee retention will benefit from this effort.

▲ **Strategy 61:** Just Ask!

The most direct way I know of to gain insight into why people are leaving your organization is to *ask them.* Exit interviews are the logical time to gather this information. I recommend the use of open-ended questions to allow the departing employee maximum flexibility in his or her response:

- "What factors influenced your decision to leave?"
- "What did you like most about your position?"
- "What did you like least?"
- "How might we improve so as to not lose others like you in the future?"
- "Is there anything else you care to share with me regarding this decision?"

You may also wish to give exiting employees a number of options regarding the exit interview format—for example, face-to-face, hard copy, or online via the Internet. Be sure to clarify that all information will be treated as confidential—that is, you will summarize information so as not to reveal its source. In other words, clarify your intent to use the information for the company's improvement without jeopardizing the exiting employee's reputation with former peers or managers. Remember, former employees typically do not want to burn their bridges behind them—if only to ensure a good reference.

Information gathered during each exit interview is an invaluable source of constructive criticism that may be applied to improving employee retention.

▲ **Strategy 62:** Exit Interviews (Revisited)

You may wish to consider applying the previously discussed exit interview methodology to new employees. In other words, take time to gather information regarding the reasons your new employees left their former employer. This information is typically gathered at some point during the interview process. It is generally handled as an informal question: "I'm curious, why are you leaving your present employer?" You may want to gather the information in a more formal manner—perhaps as a separate questionnaire within your application packet. You might ask the following questions:

- "What factors influenced your decision to leave your current or last employer?"
- "What did you like most about that position?"
- "What did you like least?"
- "Is there anything else you care to share with us regarding your decision to leave?"

You may also want to make this a *voluntary* questionnaire. To the extent that applicants are willing to share such information, you will gain insight into issues and concerns that influence employees' decisions to leave their employers. In all likelihood, these same issues and concerns will influence employees at your organization. This heads-up approach to anticipating potential problem areas may help you proactively avoid them. An ounce of retention-related problem prevention is worth a pound of cure.

▲ **Strategy 63:** Golden Handcuffs

Many companies rely on long-term financial incentives to encourage employee retention. These so-called golden handcuffs may take a variety of forms:

- Year-end rather than monthly or quarterly bonus monies
- Aggressive 401(k) matching schedule with maximum vesting schedule
- Additional qualified/nonqualified retirement programs
- Vacation days (greater seniority equals increased vacation)
- Profit and/or gain sharing
- Employee stock purchase programs

Be creative. The idea here is to tie specific financial (or other) rewards to future payout schedules. Retention will be positively affected when personnel are reluctant to walk away from the future rewards that await them.

We have all heard that "where there's a will, there's a way." Professional headhunters have the will to identify individuals within your company whose credentials and experience match those that their clients are looking for. Believe me, they will also find a way to do so.

Throughout the many years that I personally worked as a headhunter, I took great pride in telling my clients, "If you can describe what you're looking for, I can find it!" Here are some of my favorite tricks of the trade.

Voicemail 007

I would intentionally call companies after hours. I would do this in a deliberate attempt to access voicemail. When the automated operator said:

> "Welcome to XYZ Company voicemail. If you know the extension of the party you are trying to reach, PRESS 1."
>
> "If you know the name of the party you are trying to reach, PRESS 2 to *access our company directory*."

I would generally smile and think to myself "gotcha!" as I pressed "2" and prepared to transcribe the entire personnel roster of the hapless organization I had targeted. *Note:* By the way, it's not necessary to know anyone's name prior to accessing most voicemail directories. Simply press a letter and wait. Often the voicemail system will begin to rattle off names. For those systems that require the first three letters of the person's first or last name, input common names such as Smith, Johnson, Williams,

Jones, or Brown (these five names are the most common surnames in the United States, according to the U.S. Census Bureau). The first three letters of Smith will identify the voicemail of every Smith, Smithers, Smiley, and so forth in the directory. "W-I-L" yields Wilson, Willett, Wilma, and William, and so on.

Once I managed to access even a single name I could generally secure the rest. By noting the extension of the first individual I had identified, I would then work my way numerically forward and backward. For example, if John Smith was at extension 37152, I would dial extensions 37153, 37154, 37155, and so on and make note of the employee names as provided by the voicemail system. I would then call the receptionist during regular business hours to secure titles and correct spelling of names. "I am updating my records and I have John Smith's extension as 37152. Is that correct (I already know that it is)? Thank you! What is his exact title please?"

You may want to review *your* voicemail system to enhance security and not fall victim to this technique as applied by recruiters attempting to raid your organization.

Website Research

Some corporate websites contain detailed information regarding employee names, titles, and contact information. Headhunters use this information to gain insight into these organizations. For example, once upon a time, I would take the names of employees that I had identified via my "voicemail 007" technique and plug them into the internal search function of the particular company's website. This would bring up articles or Web pages referring to these specific employees. When I did not know names or contact numbers for the organization, I would use the CONTACT

Us link to identify headquarter and field office phone numbers and personnel. I would then call those numbers after hours for direct access to their voicemail system and play another round of voicemail 007. Finally, I would search the "News Release," "About Us," and other sections of the website. Companies generally include corporate brag sheet sections throughout their websites. These sections often feature valuable information regarding company, products, programs, and personnel.

I mention my war stories here to encourage you to review your website for its headhunter-raiding vulnerabilities.

Association Directories

Most associations publish membership directories. These directories are gold mines for headhunters. Believe it or not—and like it or not—it is relatively easy to secure a copy of almost any association's directory. In fact, many associations rent or sell their directories to anyone willing to pay the asking price (usually minimal). Take steps to make sure your employees are aware that any information they provide to associations may fall into the hands of headhunters and competitors. Again, you may not wish to do anything about this. Given the choice, perhaps you may wish to request that contact information be released to association members on a *need to know* basis—that is, request that your personnel not be included in public directories.

Review areas of potential vulnerability to outside raiding of your employees and take reasonable steps to avoid unnecessary risk.

⚠ **Strategy 65:** Culture

I highly recommend the book *Fish! A Remarkable Way to Boost Morale and Improve Results* by Stephen C. Lundin, Harry Paul, and John Christensen. It's a quick and enjoyable read. The *Fish!* philosophy is based on four central tenets, including, *play* (incorporating childlike spontaneity and fun into the workplace), *make their day* (a commitment to truly *delighting* the customer), *be there* (be fully present in the moment), and *choose your attitude* (positive attitude is always a matter of choice). I mention the *Fish!* philosophy in the context of employee retention concerns in that happy and successful employees tend to stay put.

I recently visited a company in Chicago that had experienced tremendous retention problems over the years. As I walked in the front door, I smiled at the receptionist and wished her a good morning. My greeting was met with a mumbled "Can I help you?" If a spark had ever existed in those eyes, I suspected it had been extinguished long ago. If she had ever had the energy or inclination to care about first impressions or customer service, that too seemed a distant memory. I noticed the way other employees shuffled their feet when they walked down the hall— there was no "spring in the strategy" at this company. No smiles, no laughter, no enthusiasm or energy. Needless to say I was not surprised to learn that out of forty employees, only two had been with the company more than a year and a half. Morale was pegging empty at this company and retention followed suit.

There is no excuse for tolerating miserable, unhappy employees even if they are desperate or foolish enough to tolerate their miserable organization. Whether the *Fish!* philosophy floats your boat or not, take time to research and implement strategies to enhance morale as a critical element of your employee retention efforts.

▲ **Strategy 66:** Environment

Remember Maslow's Hierarchy of Needs theory from your Psychology 101 class? Psychologist Abraham Maslow postulated that human beings must have their basic physiological and safety needs met before they are motivated to pursue higher levels of functioning and thought.

Maslow's Hierarchy of Needs

• *Physiological Needs.* This is the most basic level of human existence. We cannot advance to higher levels of functioning until our physiological needs have been met (air to breathe, food to eat, water to drink, sex, elimination of bodily wastes, avoidance of pain, and more).

• *Safety/Security/Order.* Once basic physiological needs are met, humans become interested in issues of protection and stability.

• *Social Needs (Affection/Belonging/Love).* Giving and receiving affection, affiliation with others, being socially wanted and accepted.

• *Esteem/Ego Needs.* Self-value and esteem of others (reputation and prestige); approval and recognition by self and others for competence and achievements.

• *The Need to Know and Understand.* To explore and comprehend, to appreciate symmetry, order, and beauty.

• *Self-Actualization.* Self-fulfillment and realization of one's potential by doing what you were born to do. Maslow believed "a musician must make music, an artist must paint, and a poet must write, if he is to be ultimately happy. What a man can be, he must be."

Whether we subscribe to Maslow's theory or not, common sense alone suggests that our employee retention objectives would be served by answering the question: How well does our work environment meet our employees' fundamental needs?

CHAPTER 6

Recruiting Excellence Workbook

In this, the final chapter of *101 Strategies for Recruiting Success,* I'd like to review much of what we've discussed thus far by way of thirty-five daily homework assignments. I encourage you to set aside time to actually do each exercise to develop your personal, day-by-day, disciplined approach to recruiting excellence. As always, I encourage you to be creative.

My wife, Gayle, is a professional artist. She often reminds her art students, "The more creatively you work day-to-day, the more frequently creative solutions will occur to you!"

This is as true in business as it is in art. Use the "Your Thoughts" section on each page to write your personal observations, notes, and brainstorming ideas.

▲ **Strategy 67 (Day 1):** Conduct a Performance *Self*-Appraisal

- What do you do well?
- Where might you improve?
- What specific steps will you commit to for improving?
- How will you measure success?

YOUR THOUGHTS:

_____

_____

_____

_____

_____

_____

_____

_____

_____

_____

_____

_____

_____

_____

_____

_____

_____

_____

_____

_____

_____

▲ **Strategy 68 (Day 2):** Read a Good Book

Better yet, read a *great* book! I recently read *Leadership,* by Rudolph Giuliani. Chapters such as "Prepare Relentlessly," "Loyalty: The Vital Virtue," and "Organize Around a Purpose" offer inspiring and useful lessons that may be readily applied personally and professionally. Read Colin Powell's *My American Journey.* Read *Fish! A Remarkable Way to Boost Morale and Improve Results* by Stephen C. Lundin, Harry Paul, and John Christensen.

Take time to expose yourself to new ideas and different points of view. What book will you start reading today? Don't procrastinate. Read a chapter over your lunch break, read another during your train ride home or before going to bed at night. What are you learning? How might you apply this knowledge?

YOUR THOUGHTS:

_____

_____

_____

_____

_____

_____

_____

_____

_____

_____

_____

_____

▲ **Strategy 69 (Day 3):** Schedule Your Next Vacation

Take a vacation sometime in the next ninety days. Plan it today!

As your schedule permits, take a long weekend or a week off (the longer the better as it generally takes a few days just to unwind). Get out of town. Lie on a beach. Hike in the woods or take in a couple of Broadway shows. Turn off your cell phone and pager. You can leave a number where family, friends, and the boss can reach you in an emergency. So, where are you headed?

The ability to balance life and work is essential to your personal and professional health.

YOUR THOUGHTS:

_____

_____

_____

_____

_____

_____

_____

_____

_____

_____

_____

_____

_____

_____

_____

_____

_____

_____

▲ **Strategy 70 (Day 4):** Interview Employees for Whom You Paid a Fee

Review your files and make a list of all employees for whom your company paid a fee. In other words, find the employees that were hired via third-party recruiters or research firms. Ask them questions such as:

- "How is it that ABC Recruiting/Research firm found you?"
- "Did they find your résumé on the Web?"
- "Did you respond to an ad?"
- "If so, do you recall where that ad was placed?"

This is a simple yet effective way to pick up on new or overlooked sourcing techniques.

YOUR THOUGHTS:

_____

_____

_____

_____

_____

_____

_____

_____

_____

_____

_____

▲ **Strategy 71 (Day 5):** Meet with Legal Counsel

Introduce yourself to legal counsel and schedule a meeting (a series of meetings may be necessary) to go over legal concerns related to the recruiting process. Review candidate screening and application procedures. Review record-keeping strategies and vendor agreements. Reviews offer letters and noncompete agreements. Develop a close working relationship with counsel to ensure legal compliance and liability-avoidance concerns have been adequately addressed.

YOUR THOUGHTS:

▲ **Strategy 72 (Day 6):** Write a Thank-You Letter

As previously mentioned, *partnering* is the confluence of relationships and resources in pursuit of a common goal.

Relationships are our personal and professional lifeblood. Don't take them for granted. Take time to write a personal thank-you note to an administrative assistant whom you rely on. Write a letter of appreciation to a hiring manager or legal counsel. Thank your boss, your peers, and your spouse. Thank your mentor. Thank your parents. Develop a habit of expressing gratitude. Little gestures of appreciation go a long way toward building solid partnering relationships.

YOUR THOUGHTS:

_____

_____

_____

_____

_____

_____

_____

_____

_____

_____

_____

_____

_____

_____

▲ **Strategy 73 (Day 7):** Take a Walk

Pay attention to your health. Often, we recruiters seem to be chained to our desks. Internet research, candidate phone calls, HRIS input, e-mail, voice mail, and mountains of paperwork demand hour upon hour of chair time. Get in the habit of taking an occasional fifteen-minute break. Weather permitting, go outside and breathe some fresh air. Walk around the block. Stand up, stretch, and clear your mind.

Take care of yourself. Diet, exercise, sleep, and a good life/work balance are critical to your fitness for the long race toward excellence.

YOUR THOUGHTS:

_____

_____

_____

_____

_____

_____

_____

_____

_____

_____

_____

_____

_____

_____

_____

▲ **Strategy 74 (Day 8):** Seek Advice

Call your mentor, a friend, a peer, or your boss. E-mail a hiring manager or legal counsel. Reach out to others with a specific request for assistance. For example, you might ask:

- "I'm trying to get a handle on the various types of immigration visas. I'd sure appreciate your advice."
- "I'm struggling with my days-to-fill ratio. You always seem to keep yours well within our targeted time frame. I'd really appreciate your advice regarding how I might improve."

Generally, people are flattered when we seek their advice. It's an opportunity to feel needed and knowledgeable. They acquire a personal stake in our success. On the other hand, we are the beneficiaries of their wisdom. It's a win-win proposition.

YOUR THOUGHTS:

_____

_____

_____

_____

_____

_____

_____

_____

_____

_____

_____

▲ Strategy 75 (Day 9): Look in the Mirror

I once knew a recruiter who kept a small mirror next to her telephone. Whenever she talked on the phone, she could see herself in that mirror. My friend was not vain. She told me that a trainer had recommended the practice as a reminder that candidates can "hear" a smile over the phone. Likewise, they can hear frustration, fatigue, or a bad mood. The mirror allows her to *see* what the person on the other end of the line is *hearing*.

Try it! Place a mirror by your phone as a reminder to convey an energetic, positive, and friendly image over the phone.

YOUR THOUGHTS:

_____

_____

_____

_____

_____

_____

_____

_____

_____

_____

_____

_____

_____

_____

_____

_____

▲ **Strategy 76 (Day 10):** Inspirational Sayings and Posters

Visit your local bookstore or mall. Look for inspirational photographs, posters, or objects. Plug the words *excellence, inspiration,* and *poster* (no quotation marks) in your favorite search engine and see what you can find.

This Yahoo search yields thousands of hits. Check out the first few. You'll be pleasantly surprised. The very first hit that came up in my search was http://www.allposters.com. I found an 8- by 10-inch poster for $8.99. It features a photograph of a climber atop a formidable-looking rock formation and the message: "GOALS: All Glory Comes from Daring."

If your budget is tight, write inspirational sayings on index cards and keep them by your desk. Surround yourself with inspirational and motivational images.

YOUR THOUGHTS:

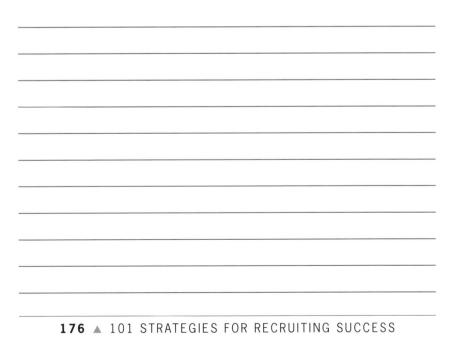

▲ Strategy 77 (Day 11): Visit the Library

Introduce yourself to the reference librarian. Familiarize yourself with library resources that may be useful to your recruiting efforts (association directories, Standard & Poor's directories, local government and community resources directories, and the like).

Check out a book on recruiting (if none are readily available ask your reference librarian to assist you with an interlibrary loan). Check out an inspirational book. Browse the business section for titles that grab your attention.

YOUR THOUGHTS:

_____

_____

_____

_____

_____

_____

_____

_____

_____

_____

_____

_____

_____

_____

_____

_____

▲ Strategy 78 (Day 12): Connect with SHRM

Visit the Society for Human Resource Management website at
http://www.shrm.org. Familiarize yourself with its programs and
services. If you're not already a member, I recommend that you
join SHRM as well as one or more of its professional emphasis
groups such as the Recruiting & Staffing Focus Area (formerly
the Employment Management Association [EMA]) at http://www
.shrm.org/ema/.

Attend local, regional, and national meetings and seminars
whenever possible to expand your knowledge and expand your
personal network within our profession.

YOUR THOUGHTS:

_____

_____

_____

_____

_____

_____

_____

_____

_____

_____

_____

_____

_____

▲ **Strategy 79 (Day 13):** Call a Candidate Who Rejected You

There are valuable lessons to be learned when things don't go our way. Track down a few candidates that your company had interest in who did not choose to pursue the opportunity. Give them a call and reintroduce yourself. Tell them that you are always looking for ways to improve yourself and your company. Then state something along the lines of: "I'm hoping you might spare a few minutes of your time to answer a few questions related to your recent experience with my company." Then, ask the following questions:

- "What were the positive aspects of your experience with our recruiting efforts?"
- "Where might we improve?"
- "What factors influenced your decision regarding this opportunity?"
- "May I stay in touch with you regarding future opportunities?"

YOUR THOUGHTS:

_____

_____

_____

_____

_____

_____

_____

▲ Strategy 80 (Day 14): Be a Team Player

Recruiting is a team sport! Success depends on the coordinated efforts of everyone involved in the process: recruiters, research assistants, hiring managers, IT support personnel, senior management, and others.

Take a few moments to list the names and roles of the team members you rely on. Schedule brainstorming meetings with these individuals. Thank them for helping you. Ask them. "What can I do to help *you* succeed?"

YOUR THOUGHTS:

_____

_____

_____

_____

_____

_____

_____

_____

_____

_____

_____

_____

_____

_____

_____

_____

_____

▲ **Strategy 81 (Day 15):** Read Your Annual Report

We often get so focused on our personal niche within the company that we fail to take time to gain a broader perspective. Sit down with a highlighter and your most recent annual report and other brochures or collateral material. Review the material carefully.

Take time to gain big picture insight into your organization.

YOUR THOUGHTS:

▲ **Strategy 82 (Day 16):** Set a New Goal

Challenge yourself with a new stretch goal, such as one of the following:

- I will reduce my days-to-fill ratio by 25 percent in the next ninety days.
- I will earn SPHR or PHR certification within the next six months.
- I will reduce my reliance on outside recruiters by 50 percent.
- I will read two or more motivational or educational books each month.

Excellence begins with goal setting.

YOUR THOUGHTS:

_____

_____

_____

_____

_____

_____

_____

_____

_____

_____

_____

▲ **Strategy 83 (Day 17):** Attend a Seminar or Take a Class

What SHRM or other professional seminars and workshops are available to you in the near future? Perhaps a local high school or college is offering a continuing education course that peaks your interest. Maybe a guest lecture at the library or local university is open to the public. Expose yourself to new ideas. Expand your worldview. Learn, discover, and grow.

YOUR THOUGHTS:

▲ **Strategy 84 (Day 18):** Brainstorm

Set aside at least fifteen to twenty minutes of quiet time each day to brainstorm. Tackle one topic at a time:

- What new sourcing techniques can I think of?
- What expenses can I eliminate or reduce to improve cost-per-hire?
- What can I do to achieve greater work/life balance?
- How might I solve this problem?

Regular brainstorming is an effective rut-busting technique.

YOUR THOUGHTS:

_____

_____

_____

_____

_____

_____

_____

_____

_____

_____

_____

_____

_____

▲ **Strategy 85 (Day 19):** Off-Site Meetings

Speaking of ruts, make it a point to get away from the office occasionally. Rent or borrow off-site space for a team meeting where you will be free from typical distractions. Bring in a guest speaker. Engage in team-building exercises and group brainstorming sessions. Invite the members of your team to prepare special-topic presentations.

An occasional change of scenery encourages new perspectives.

YOUR THOUGHTS:

_____

_____

_____

_____

_____

_____

_____

_____

_____

_____

_____

_____

_____

_____

_____

_____

▲ **Strategy 86 (Day 20):** Take a Loved One to Lunch

Busy days turn into busy weeks, months, and years. It's easy to get so caught up in our professional duties that we neglect personal relationships. Take a loved one to lunch from time to time. I suggest you discipline yourself to maintain a minimum once-per-month luncheon date. Invite your spouse, your son or daughter, parents, or a dear friend. An occasional break from professional routine to connect with loved ones is vital to work/life balance and the maintenance of healthy interpersonal relationships.

YOUR THOUGHTS:

_____

_____

_____

_____

_____

_____

_____

_____

_____

_____

_____

_____

_____

_____

_____

_____

▲ **Strategy 87 (Day 21):** Count Your Blessings

Daily pressures and challenges can affect our attitude, energy, sense of well-being, and our health. Take a fifteen-to-twenty-minute break at some point in your day to count your blessings.

Relax, and enjoy thinking about the people, activities, and things in life that are your greatest sources of pleasure and fulfillment.

YOUR THOUGHTS:

_____

_____

_____

_____

_____

_____

_____

_____

_____

_____

_____

_____

_____

_____

_____

_____

_____

_____

_____

▲ **Strategy 88 (Day 22):** Interview a Client

Call one of your clients and schedule a meeting for the sole purpose of learning more about his or her area of expertise. You might ask the following questions:

- "Please give me an overview of your group's areas of responsibility."
- "What does your typical day look like?"
- "What associations do people in your profession tend to belong to?"
- "What professional journals do you read?"
- "What current and anticipated challenges does your group face?"
- "How might recruiting best support your group?"

Crawl into your client's world!

YOUR THOUGHTS:

_____

_____

_____

_____

_____

_____

_____

_____

▲ **Strategy 89 (Day 23):** Fill Out an Application

Put yourself in the candidate's shoes for a moment. Fill out a copy of your company's employment application form (hard copy and online versions).

- Is the application user-friendly?
- Are the instructions clear?
- Is each section necessary?
- How might the form be improved?

YOUR THOUGHTS:

_____

_____

_____

_____

_____

_____

_____

_____

_____

_____

_____

_____

_____

_____

_____

_____

_____

_____

▲ **Strategy 90 (Day 24):** Visit Your Company's Website

Again, take a candidate's perspective as you examine your company's website.

- Is it easy to find the career section?
- Is it easy to search open jobs?
- Is navigation user-friendly and intuitive?
- How might the site be modified or improved?

Schedule a meeting with your website administrator to review your findings and suggest improvements.

YOUR THOUGHTS:

_____

_____

_____

_____

_____

_____

_____

_____

_____

_____

_____

_____

_____

_____

_____

▲ **Strategy 91 (Day 25):** Visit a Competitor's Website

Visit your competitors' websites.

- How do competitor websites compare with your company's website?
- Are there things you may wish to incorporate into your site?
- Are there things you'll want to avoid?

YOUR THOUGHTS:

_____

_____

_____

_____

_____

_____

_____

_____

_____

_____

_____

_____

_____

_____

_____

▲ **Strategy 92 (Day 26):** Visit Internet Job Sites

Visit a number of the major job boards such as:

- Monster Board (http://www.monster.com)
- Careerbuilder (http://www.careerbuilder.com/)
- HotJobs (http://www.hotjobs.com)

Review job advertisements regarding positions that appear to be similar to those you typically have on your plate. Pay attention to how your competitors and third-party recruiters word their advertisements and which boards they use.

What have you learned?

YOUR THOUGHTS:

_____

_____

_____

_____

_____

_____

_____

_____

_____

_____

_____

_____

_____

▲ **Strategy 93 (Day 27):** Interview Other Recruiters

Call peers within your own company as well those at competitors and third-party vendors whom you respect. A flattering opener is, "In my efforts to develop as a recruiter I thought I'd contact a few recruiters whom I personally respect and seek their advice. May I ask you a few questions?" As such, it's hard to say no to it.

- "What recruiting techniques are most effective for you?"
- "If you were looking for an individual with _____ skills, how would you go about finding such a person?"
- "What is the secret of your success?"

Be sure to thank participants for their assistance and invite them to call on you anytime you can return a favor.

YOUR THOUGHTS:

_____

_____

_____

_____

_____

_____

_____

_____

_____

_____

_____

▲ **Strategy 94 (Day 28):** Visit a Career Fair

Visit a career fair from the candidate's perspective. Take time to visit booths and critique why certain booths (and recruiters) are better than others.

- What lessons have you learned?
- What new ideas might you try?
- What should you avoid?

YOUR THOUGHTS:

_____

_____

_____

_____

_____

_____

_____

_____

_____

_____

_____

_____

_____

_____

_____

_____

▲ Strategy 95 (Day 29): Critique Your Tools

Do you work for your tools or do they work for you? Take a critical look at your HRIS system. Is it user-friendly or cumbersome? Do you spend too much time inputting versus retrieving information? If so, how might you improve its design? What tasks can or should be off-loaded to administrative support personnel? Take a critical look at résumé databases you subscribe to. Look at your voicemail and e-mail services. Look at the desktop software you utilize throughout your day.

What modifications or changes might you make to improve functionality and efficiency?

YOUR THOUGHTS:

_____

_____

_____

_____

_____

_____

_____

_____

_____

_____

_____

_____

_____

_____

_____

▲ **Strategy 96 (Day 30):** Study Time Management

Enroll in a time management course. Alternatively, check out a number of books on the topic to find the time management system that works best for you. An Internet search for *"Time Management" best practices* will point you in the right direction.

YOUR THOUGHTS:

▲ **Strategy 97 (Day 31):** Plan Your Day

Apply lessons learned via your time management study to the task of planning your day. Before you head home in the evening, plan the following day's activities. This will help ensure effective prioritization of your workload. Unanticipated interruptions and change of plans may arise from time to time. You may need to modify your schedule as necessary. In general, a planned day tends to be a productive day.

YOUR THOUGHTS:

▲ **Strategy 98 (Day 32):** Seek Out a Mentor

Ask a professional whom you respect and admire if he or she will be your personal mentor. A mentor will be someone who agrees to meet with you on a regular basis to facilitate your professional success (for example, a one-hour meeting once every week or two). He or she will be an on-call sounding board. He or she will provide guidance and instruction to help you along your career path. Chances are your would-be mentor has had a mentor himself or herself along the way. He or she will typically be flattered that you are interested in this type of relationship. If unwilling or unable to personally fill such a role, perhaps he or she will be willing to recommend others.

Write the names of your top three mentor prospects. Approach each in turn until you have established a mentor relationship.

YOUR THOUGHTS:

_____

_____

_____

_____

_____

_____

_____

_____

_____

_____

▲ **Strategy 99 (Day 33):** Be a Mentor

A well-known adage states that "the teacher learns as much as the student." Actively pursue or create an opportunity to become a mentor yourself.

YOUR THOUGHTS:

_____

_____

_____

_____

_____

_____

_____

_____

_____

_____

_____

_____

_____

_____

_____

_____

_____

_____

_____

_____

_____

▲ **Strategy 100 (Day 34):** Conduct an Operational Audit

As noted in Chapter 1, a comprehensive audit of recruiting policies, procedures, tools, and personnel should be undertaken to determine departmental strengths and weaknesses. Using the aforementioned text as your guide, initiate an operational audit of work flow, competency, and support functions within your recruitment operations.

YOUR THOUGHTS:

▲ **Strategy 101 (Day 35):** Take These Lessons to Heart

By now, you have begun to develop your own answer to the question asked in Strategy 1 of our journey toward recruiting excellence: What is a recruiter? Reread this text from time to time. Take time to answer the questions raised and complete suggested exercises. Rise above mediocrity and count yourself among those rare professionals who are engaged in the relentless pursuit of excellence.

YOUR THOUGHTS:

Index

accounting firms, recruitment by, 57
administrators, as recruiters, 5
adverse impact, 118
African-American associations and organizations, 100
Age Discrimination in Employment Act of 1967, 118, 130, 136
alliances between recruiters, 78–79
alumni associations, 62–63
alumni newsletter, corporate, 57
American Society for Training and Development, 50
Americans with Disabilities Act of 1990, 130, 136
anti-raiding strategies, 160–162
Association of Career Firms International, 43
associations
    African-American, 100
    disability-related, 101
    Hispanic and Latino, 101
    membership directories, 162
    sexual-orientation, 101–102

audit, operational, 7–9, 200
average (statistics), 18–19

background checking, 133–134
balancing life and work, 169
behavioral interviewing, 128–129
blended service model, 2
blind advertisement, 30
brainstorming, 184
Bureau of Citizenship and Immigration Services, 83
Business Publication Advertising Source, 48

candidate pipeline, 87–88
career fairs, 44–45, 194
certification preparation programs, 65
checklist, for new hires, 142–143
Christensen, John, *Fish! A Remarkable Way to Boost Morale and Improve Results*, 163

Civil Rights Act of 1964, 118, 129
    Title VII claims, 93
Civil Rights Act of 1991, 130
classified advertising, 48–49
clients of recruiters
    feedback from, 33–34
    learning about, 31–32
closed-ended questions, 129
collateral material, 132
colleges
    alumni associations, 62–63
    recruiting at, 59–61
    United Negro College Fund,
        98–100
committees, employee participation,
    149–150
community building, 145
community meetings, 150
community resources, 53–54
compensation, for recruitment, 6
competitors, as recruiting source,
    78–80
contingency fees, appropriate rate,
    23–24
contingency recruiter, 71–72
    vs. retained search firms, 22
continuing education programs, 65
contracts, with third-party recruiters,
    24–25
cost-per-hire, 17–18, 37
culture, and employee retention, 144,
    163
customer satisfaction survey, 33–34

data capture, simplifying, 15–16
databases, 15
    evaluating, 195
days-to-fill, 18–21
Defense Authorization Act (1991), 67
Defense Outplacement Referral Sys-
    tem, 67

deliverables, 28
development, training and, 12–13,
    151
Devry Institute, 64
direct sourcing, 78
directories, of associations, 162
disability-related associations, 101
discrimination
    cost of, 94–95
    legal restrictions, 129–130
diversity
    attracting and retaining diverse tal-
        ent, 92–103
    organizational acceptance, 103
downsizing, and sourcing, 89

e-mail accounts, for résumés, 29
employees
    interviewing those found by re-
        cruiters, 170
    measuring satisfaction, 153–154
    performance appraisal, 155–156
    reasons for turnover, 157
    referrals by, 55–56, 149
    website for information on,
        161–162
employment application form,
    123–127
    locating on website, 125
    user-friendly, 126–127
environment, and employee reten-
    tion, 164–165
Equal Employment Opportunity
    Commission, 130
Equal Pay Act of 1963, 130, 136
Equipment Lessor Association, 50
esteem in Maslow's hierarchy, 164
evaluation
    of company website, 190
    of databases, 195

of hiring process, 138–139
time management, 196
exit interviews, 57, 157–158

Fair Chance, 94
Fair Labor Standards Act, 136
feedback
from clients, 33–34
in hiring process, 114–115
Find-a-Firm directory, 43
first impressions, 117
Fish! A Remarkable Way to Boost Morale and Improve Results (Lundin, Paul, Christensen), 163

Giuliani, Rudolph, *Leadership*, 168
goals, setting, 182
golden handcuffs, 159
government resources, 46

headhunters, strategies, 160–162
hiring
administrative procedures, 112
decision process, 115
employment application form, 123–127
evaluation, 138–139
feedback in process, 114–115
interview, 128–131
offer, 135
paperwork, 136–137
partnering, 107–108
promises made, 152
screening candidates, 113
see also interview process
hiring manager
candidate introduction to, 113–114
partnering with, 107–108
Hirsh, Christine, on recruiting research, 69–70
Hispanic associations, 101

Immigration Reform and Control Act, 136
information storage and retrieval system, 15
inspirational sayings and posters, 176
internal postings and promotions, 85–86
international recruiting, sourcing and, 83–84
Internet
job sites, 192
search engine queries, 65–66
interview process, 27, 128–131
background and reference checking, 133–134
client, 188
collateral material, 132
involvement, and employee retention, 149–150
ITT Technical Institute, 64

job applications
evaluating, 189
résumé availability, 14–15
job candidates
managing flow, 29–30
offer, 135
pre-closing for hiring authority, 120–121
screening, 113, 118–119
sharing offer or notice of rejection, 115–116
those who rejected you, 179
Job Search, 67
journals, classified advertising in, 48–49

KISS rule, 14–16

Latino associations, 101
layoffs, and sourcing, 89
Leadership (Giuliani), 168

legal counsel, meeting with, 171
libraries, 46, 177
Lincoln Training Center, 47
"low-hanging fruit," 14
Lundin, Stephen *Fish! A Remarkable Way to Boost Morale and Improve Results*, 163

magazines, classified advertising in, 48–49
Management Recruiters (MRI), 1
Maritz Rewards, 148
Maslow's Hierarchy of Needs, 164
mean (statistics), 19
media, 41–42
media kit, 48
median (statistics), 19
mediocrity, 1
meetings
    community, 150
    need for regular, 35–36
    off-site, 185
mentoring, 144, 174, 198, 199
metrics, 17–21
military outplacement, 67–68
mirror, 175
mode (statistics), 19
morale, 163
motivational sayings, 176
My American Journey (Powell), 168

National Committee on Pay Equity, 94
negotiating recruitment fees, 23–24
networking, 81–82
newsgroups, help-wanted postings to, 51
newspaper advertising, 41–42
nonworking days, and days-to-fill statistic, 19–20
North American Free Trade Agreement, 83–84

objectives, clarity in, 28
offer, 135
offer-to-acceptance ratio, 38
off-site meetings, 185
onboarding, 142–143
open houses, 75–77
open-ended questions, 129
    in exit interview, 157
Operation Transition, 67
operational audit, 7–9, 200
operational success strategies
    baseline, 37–38
    candidate flow management, 29–30
    deliverables, 28
    metrics, 17–21
    operational audit, 7–9
    organization charts, 39–40
    planning, 10–11
    recruiters' duties, 4–6
    regular meetings and reports, 35–36
    simplicity, 14–16
    training and development, 12–13
    understanding process, 26–27
    vendor relationship management, 22–25
    working relationships, 31–32
optical character recognition (OCR), 15
optimal recruiter, 5–6
organization charts, 39–40
organizations, African-American, 100
outplacement, 43
outside recruiters (third-party recruiting), 6, 14
    contracts, 24–25
outsourcing, background and reference checking, 133–134

partnering, with hiring manager, 107–108

Paul, Harry, *Fish! A Remarkable Way to Boost Morale and Improve Results*, 163
pay equity, 94
peer relationships, 78–79
performance, baseline measurements and, 37–38
performance appraisal, 155–156
performance self-appraisal, 167
personal relationships, 186
physical exercise, 173
physiological needs in Maslow's hierarchy, 164
pipeline, 87–88
planning, 10–11, 197
posting jobs internally, 85–86
Powell, Colin, *My American Journey*, 168
preparations for new employee, 142
prioritizing requisition, 111–112
promises, 152
promotions, internal, 85–86
protected classes, 118

questions in interview, open- or closed-ended, 129

recognition and rewards, 146–148
recruiters
    duties, 4–6
    interviewing other, 193
    outside(third-party), *see* third-party recruiting industry
recruiting process, 117–122
    follow-through, 121–122
    initial contact, 117–118
    interviewing employees found by, 170
    planning, 117
    pre-closing candidates, 120–121
    selling opportunity, 119–120
reference checking, 133–134

referrals by employees, 55–56, 149
refreshments, for open houses, 76
Rehabilitation Act of 1973, 130
rejection letter for job candidate, 115–116, 121
relationships, 172
report card, and employee retention, 153–154
reports, need for regular, 35–36
requisition
    assignment to recruiter, 110–111
    closing, 27
    opening, 26, 109–110
    prioritizing, 111–112
research firms, 69–70
résumés
    availability, 14–15
    managing flow, 29–30
retained search firms, 73–74
    decision to use, 22
retention, 140–141
    anti-raiding strategies, 160–162
    community building, 145
    culture, 163
    environment, 164–165
    exit interviews, 157–158
    golden handcuffs, 159
    involvement, 149–150
    mentoring, 144
    onboarding, 142–143
    performance appraisal, 155–156
    promises, 152
    recognition and rewards, 146–148
    report card, 153–154
    training and development, 151
rewards, and employee retention, 159

safety/security/order in Maslow's hierarchy, 164
scanner, 15
screening candidates, 26–27, 113, 118–119

search engine queries, refining, 65–66
"seat at the table," 31–32
self-actualization in Maslow's hierarchy, 164
seminars, 183
sexual-orientation associations, 101–102
simplicity, 14–16
social needs in Maslow's hierarchy, 164
social services, 47
Society for Human Resource Management, 50, 178
sourcing, 26, 112–113
  alumni associations, 62–63
  associations, 50–52
  brainstorming, 90–91
  candidate pipeline, 87–88
  career fairs, 44–45
  college and university recruiting, 59–61
  community resources, 53–54
  company alumni, 57–58
  competitors, 78–80
  contingency recruiter, 71–72
  employee referrals, 55–56
  government resources, 46
  internal postings and promotions, 85–86
  international recruiting and, 83–84
  media, 41–42
  military outplacement, 67–68
  networking, 81–82
  nontraditional schools and programs, 64–66
  open houses and other events, 75–77
  outplacement, 43
  professional journals and magazines, 48–49
  research firms, 69–70

retained search firms, 73–74
roadkill, 89
  social services, 47
spam, help-wanted postings as, 51
split business, 78
staffing, for open houses, 76
Standard Rate and Data Service (SRDS), 48
status quo, diversity and, 93, 96–97
stress, cost of, 95
submissions-to-candidates statistic, 20–21
submission-to-hire ratio, 38

target deliverables, 37
technical institutes, 64–65
technologies, user groups, 50–51
telephone, image over, 175
testing, 113
  prescreening, 118
thank you letter, 172
third-party recruiting industry, 6, 14
  contracts, 24–25
time management, evaluation, 196
time-stamp, for requisition, 110
training and development, 12–13, 151

Unemployment bureau, 46
United Negro College Fund, colleges, 98–100
U.S. Bureau of Citizenship and Immigration Services, 83
universities
  alumni associations, 62–63
  recruiting at, 59–61
user-friendly employment application form, 126–127
user groups, help-wanted postings as, 51

vacation, 169

vendor relationship management,
22–25

voicemail, 160

websites

employee information on, 161–162

evaluating company's, 190

viewing competitor's, 191

work visas, 83

workbook exercises, 166

annual report, 181

application form, 189

book reading, 168

brainstorming, 184

career fairs, 194

counting blessings, 187

evaluating tools, 195

goal setting, 182

image over telephone, 175

inspirational sayings and posters,
176

interviewing client, 188

interviewing other recruiters, 193

job candidates who rejected you,
179

legal counsel meeting, 171

libraries, 177

mentoring, 198, 199

off-site meetings, 185

operational audit, 200

performance self-appraisal, 167

personal relationships, 186

planning, 197

scheduling vacation, 169

seeking advice, 174

seminars, 183

Society for Human Resources
Management, 178

teamwork, 180

thank you letter, 172

time management, 196

viewing websites, 190–191

walk, 173

websites for job hunting, 192

workflow, for recruiting operations, 7

working relationships, 31–32

workload balancing, 111

Workstream, Inc., 69